# TABE OF CONTENTS

Introduction .................................................. 1
CHAPTER 1 ................................................... 2
CHAPTER 2 ................................................... 5

Insights on Stabilizing Appetite and Energy Levels ............ 5
CHAPTER 3 ................................................... 7
CHAPTER 4 ................................................... 11
Incorporating Physical Activity for Golo Benefits ............. 11
CHAPTER 5 ................................................... 14
Getting Started with the Golo Diet ........................... 14
CHAPTER 6 ................................................... 20
Adapting the GOLO Diet for Different Life Stages ............. 20

**Breakfast** .................................................. 23
    Protein-Packed Omelette ................................ 23
    Quinoa Breakfast Bowl .................................. 23
    Banana Nut Overnight Oats .............................. 24
    Veggie Breakfast Burrito ............................... 25
    Overnight Oats with Berries ............................ 25
    Egg and Veggie Scramble ................................ 26
    Chia Pudding with Fruit ................................ 27
    Avocado Toast on Whole Grain Bread ..................... 27
    Spinach and Feta Frittata .............................. 28
    Healthy Banana Pancakes ................................ 29
    Sweet Potato Hash ...................................... 29
    Almond Milk and Oats Porridge .......................... 30

**Lunch** ..................................................... 31
    Quinoa and Black Bean Stuffed Peppers .................. 31
    Tuna Salad Stuffed Bell Peppers ........................ 31
    Black Bean and Corn Quesadillas ........................ 32
    Mushroom Barley Soup ................................... 33
    Chicken and Avocado Wrap ............................... 33

Turkey Chili with Beans .................................................. 34
Grilled Chicken Salad with Balsamic Vinaigrette ............ 35
Veggie and Hummus Sandwich ................................... 36
Stuffed Bell Peppers ..................................................... 37
Spinach and Tomato Stuffed Chicken .......................... 37
Sweet Potato and Black Bean Chili .............................. 38
Veggie and Brown Rice Stir Fry .................................... 39

**Dinner** ........................................................................ **40**
Grilled Beef Kebabs with Vegetables ........................... 40
Cauliflower Fried Rice with Tofu .................................. 41
Baked Lemon Herb Chicken with Quinoa ................... 41
Zucchini Noodles & Turkey Bolognese ........................ 42
Stuffed Portobello Mushrooms .................................... 43
Chicken & Vegetable Stir-Fry ....................................... 44
Baked Eggplant Parmesan ........................................... 44
Chicken and Vegetable Casserole ............................... 45
Quinoa and Black Bean Tacos ..................................... 46
Roasted Vegetable Pasta ............................................. 46
Teriyaki Chicken with Brown Rice ................................ 47
Hearty Vegetable Soup ................................................ 48

**Snacks** ....................................................................... **49**
Baked Zucchini Chips .................................................. 49
Roasted Chickpeas ...................................................... 50
Mango Salsa with Tortilla Chips ................................... 51
Dark Chocolate and Almond Protein Bars ................... 51
Healthy Nut Butter Rice Cakes ..................................... 52
Cucumber Rolls with Tuna Salad .................................. 52
Healthy Granola Bars ................................................... 53
Smoked Salmon Cucumber Bites ................................ 53
Zucchini Fritters with Yogurt Sauce .............................. 54
Banana-Oat Cookies .................................................... 55
Baked Kale Chips ......................................................... 56
Vanilla Protein Pancakes .............................................. 56

# GOLO DIET COOKBOOK

**FOR BEGINNERS & SENIORS**

*The Ultimate Guide to Balanced Eating with 2000 Days of Super Easy and Quick Recipes Suitable for All Ages.*
*Revitalize Your Metabolism and Lose Weight Without Sacrificing Flavor.*
**60-Day BEGINNER'S Meal Plan with Delicious Recipes.**

**By Philippa Row**

**Copyright © 2024 by Philippa Row**

All rights reserved.

It is not legal to reproduce, duplicate, or transmit any part of this document in electronic means or in printed format.

Recording of this publication is strictly prohibited, and any storage of this document is not allowed unless with written permission from the publisher, except for brief quotations in a book review.

**Dessert** .................................................... **57**
　Homemade Trail Mix .................................... 57
　Fresh Fruit Salad with Mint ............................ 57
　Greek Yogurt with Honey and Berries ............. 58
　Almond and Date Energy Bars ...................... 59
　Cocoa Banana Bread .................................... 59
　Dark Chocolate Avocado Mousse .................. 60
　Greek Yogurt Popsicles with Fresh Fruit .......... 61
　Baked Pear with Walnuts & Honey ................. 61
　Apple Cinnamon Baked Oatmeal Cups .......... 62
　Peanut Butter & Jelly Protein Bars ................. 63
　Chocolate-Dipped Coconut Macaroons ......... 63
　Mango & Coconut Rice Pudding ................... 64

**CHAPTER 7** ............................................... **65**
FAQ Section for the GOLO Diet ......................... 65
Conclusion ........................................................ 69
Recipe index ..................................................... 70
60 DAY MEAL PLAN ......................................... 72

# INTRODUCTION

Starting a healthier lifestyle is a commendable decision but sometimes can be challenging. Recipes may appear complex, ingredient lists overwhelming, and cooking techniques daunting. We understand these challenges and this cookbook help simplify all to achieve your desire result. The Cookbook stands as your trusted companion on this transformative path. Our goal is to empower you with the knowledge, tools, and delightful recipes needed to make every culinary endeavor both accessible and nourishing.

This cookbook is designed with a deep appreciation for two distinct but equally significant demographics: those who are taking their first steps on the journey to healthier living and those who have gracefully traversed the years and seek to maintain their well-being.

For beginners, this cookbook serves as a friendly and knowledgeable companion on your quest for better health. The initial steps towards healthier living can often seem like a daunting path, filled with unfamiliar ingredients, complex recipes, and contradictory dietary advice. In recognizing this, we aim to make this journey both accessible and enjoyable. You'll find a wealth of information, guidance, and recipes tailored to your needs.

For seniors, this cookbook is a tribute to the wisdom and experience that age brings. It's a testament to the belief that age is not a barrier to vibrant health and the enjoyment of delicious, nourishing meals. We understand that dietary needs change with time, and we've curated recipes that are not only nutritionally rich but also take into account the unique considerations of aging gracefully.

This book celebrates the joy of cooking, a path to better health, and a tribute to the wisdom of age. By following the principles of this program, individuals can support their overall health and well-being as they age, helping them to live a more vibrant and fulfilling life.

# CHAPTER 1
## Understanding the GOLO Diet

At the heart of our cookbook and the path to better health lies a profound and comprehensive understanding of the principles that underpin the GOLO diet. This dietary approach is not a fleeting trend but rather a science-backed, holistic method that revolves around the regulation of one fundamental hormone: insulin. To embark on a successful journey toward healthier living, it is essential to grasp the principles that guide the GOLO diet.

Insulin, a hormone that is generated by the pancreas, plays a vital role in controlling blood sugar levels and, as a result, determines whether our bodies store fat or burn it for energy. This is the fundamental premise around which the GOLO diet is founded. By gaining a solid understanding of this mechanism, individuals can unlock the potential for sustainable and long-lasting improvements in their health and well-being.

GOLO diet principles encompass a balanced and mindful approach to nutrition. It encourages individuals to make informed choices about the foods they consume, considering the impact on their insulin levels and overall health. This goes beyond mere calorie counting and restrictive eating; it's about adopting a sustainable way of nourishing the body, with a focus on nutrient-dense, whole foods.

In simple terms, the diet is a way of eating that focuses on keeping your blood sugar levels stable. It's all about choosing foods that won't cause your blood sugar to spike and crash, which can lead to cravings and overeating. The key to this diet is understanding how insulin works in your body. By eating the right foods in the right proportions, you can help your body use insulin more effectively and keep your energy levels steady.

This is not only beneficial for weight loss, but it also contributes to an improvement in overall health. In a nutshell, the GOLO diet is about making smart food choices to help you feel satisfied, energized, and in control of your eating habits.

Understanding the principles of the GOLO diet is like deciphering the code to a healthier life. It equips individuals with the knowledge and tools needed to make informed dietary choices, harnessing the power of nutrition to support overall well- being. It's about recognizing that food is not just fuel; it's a powerful influencer of our health, energy levels, and quality of life.

## How the GOLO Metabolic Plan Supports Weight Loss and Health

The GOLO Metabolic Plan serves as the practical implementation of the GOLO diet principles, providing individuals with a structured yet flexible approach to eating that supports not only weight loss but also overall health. This plan is a blueprint for achieving and maintaining balanced insulin levels, offering a sustainable path to better well-being.

At its core, the GOLO Metabolic Plan revolves around several key components, each designed to contribute to weight loss and improved metabolic health. These components include:

**Balanced Nutrition:** The plan places a strong emphasis on balanced nutrition, encouraging individuals to make mindful choices when it comes to the foods they consume. It's about nourishing the body with nutrient- dense, whole foods that support overall health and well-being.

**Portion Control:** Effective portion control is a fundamental aspect of the plan. By understanding appropriate portion sizes and practicing moderation, individuals can achieve better control over their calorie intake and reduce overconsumption.

**Regular Exercise:** Physical activity is a crucial element of the GOLO Metabolic Plan. Regular exercise not only burns calories but also helps improve insulin sensitivity, supporting better blood sugar control.

**Supportive Supplements:** The plan incorporates specific supplements designed to complement the dietary approach. These supplements are carefully selected to aid in insulin regulation and metabolic function.

**Hydration:** Proper hydration is essential for metabolic health. The plan emphasizes the importance of staying well-hydrated for optimal well-being.

By following the GOLO Metabolic Plan, individuals can embark on a journey toward improved health and sustainable weight loss. It provides a structured framework that integrates nutrition, exercise, and healthy habits into daily life. Moreover, it acknowledges that one size doesn't fit all, offering flexibility to accommodate various dietary preferences and lifestyles.

The plan encourages individuals to view food as a source of nourishment and energy rather than as a source of restriction. It promotes the idea that healthy eating can be both enjoyable and sustainable, dispelling the notion that dietary changes need to be drastic or extreme. Instead, it advocates for gradual, realistic changes that can be maintained for the long term.

Ultimately, the GOLO Metabolic Plan is not just a diet; it's a lifestyle approach to better health. It empowers individuals to take charge of their well-being, guiding them toward a balanced and sustainable path to weight loss and improved metabolic health. It's a journey that prioritizes health and vitality, one meal and one step at a time.

# CHAPTER 2
## Insights on Stabilizing Appetite and Energy Levels

Appetite and energy levels are influenced not only by what we eat and how much we eat, but also by a complex network of hormones including, but not limited to, insulin and cortisol. These hormones play a crucial role in regulating our metabolism, our sense of satiety, and our ability to effectively manage body weight.

## The Physiology of Appetite and Energy

To understand how we can stabilize appetite and energy levels through diet, it's essential to first explore the physiology behind these processes. Insulin, which is a hormone that is generated by the pancreas, has a role in the regulation of glucose levels in the blood. After a meal, carbohydrates break down into glucose, which enters the bloodstream. Insulin facilitates the entry of glucose into cells, where it can be used to produce energy. If insulin levels are too high or too low, it can lead to fluctuations in energy and appetite, contributing to long-term health issues such as type 2 diabetes and obesity.

Adrenal glands are responsible for the production of cortisol, which is also referred to as the stress hormone. In response to physical or emotional stress, cortisol releases sugars into the blood, providing an immediate energy source. If cortisol is chronically elevated, it can lead to increases in appetite, particularly for high-fat and sugary foods, which can in turn lead to weight gain and other health issues.

# Dietary Strategies for Hormonal Stabilization

### 1. Macronutrient Balance

A balanced diet that comprises the right proportion of carbohydrates, proteins, and fats can help maintain stable insulin and cortisol levels. Here are some guidelines:

- **Carbohydrates:** Opt for complex carbohydrates like quinoa, oats, legumes, and green leafy vegetables, which have a lower glycemic index and release glucose more slowly into the bloodstream. This helps avoid insulin spikes.

- **Proteins:** Incorporate lean protein sources such as chicken, turkey, fish, tofu, and legumes in every meal to help extend feelings of fullness and stabilize blood glucose levels.

- **Fats:** Comprise healthy fats from sources such as avocados, nuts, seeds, and olive oil, which not only help slow glucose absorption but can also moderate cortisol response.

### 2. Fiber-Rich Foods

Dietary fibers found in vegetables, fruits, legumes, and whole grains can slow down the digestion of food and the absorption of glucose, leading to a more gradual rise and subsequent decrease in insulin levels. Additionally, fibers help maintain a healthy gut and promote regular bowel movements, which are vital for hormonal regulation and appetite control.

### 3. Meal Frequency

Eating at regular intervals can help maintain stable energy levels and appetite. Skipping meals or fasting for long periods can lead to a lowered metabolism and a subsequent excessive response of cortisol and insulin when food is finally consumed. Ideally, meals and snacks should be planned every three to four hours.

# CHAPTER 3

## Stress Reduction and Hormonal Management

Managing stress is crucial for maintaining balanced hormone levels, which in turn influences overall health, appetite control, and energy levels. Stress, particularly chronic stress, can lead to significant disruptions in hormonal balance, impacting not only cortisol but also other hormones such as insulin, adrenaline, and ghrelin—the hunger hormone. Understanding how to manage stress and its effects on the body can play a significant role in achieving a healthy lifestyle and effective weight management.

## The Impact of Stress on Hormonal Balance

Stress activates the body's "fight or flight" response, which is intended to protect us in life-threatening situations. This response triggers the adrenal glands to release adrenaline and cortisol, which increases blood sugar levels and energy availability. While this response is vital in emergency situations, frequent activation due to chronic stress can lead to high cortisol levels. Over time, elevated cortisol can cause increased appetite and cravings for unhealthy foods, weight gain, and an increased risk of diseases like type 2 diabetes and hypertension.

## Moreover, stress can impact other hormones such as:

- **Insulin:** Insulin resistance is a condition in which the cells of the body do not respond appropriately to insulin. Stress can cause this condition making it difficult to manage blood sugar levels.

- **Ghrelin:** Known as the hunger hormone, ghrelin levels can increase under stress, leading to increased appetite and potential weight gain.

- **Leptin:** This hormone helps to regulate energy balance and inhibit hunger. Chronic stress can impair leptin's effectiveness, which can disrupt appetite signals and lead to overeating.

## Techniques for Reducing Stress

Incorporating specific stress-reduction techniques into daily life can help manage and mitigate the harmful effects of stress on hormonal balance and overall health:

### 1. Mindfulness and Meditation

Mindfulness meditation has been shown to reduce the production of stress hormones. Regular practice can help lower cortisol levels, improve insulin sensitivity, and enhance mental and emotional well-being. Being totally involved with the moment while embracing it without passing judgment on it is an essential component of mindfulness. Meditation often includes deep breathing techniques and can be practiced anywhere—from a quiet room to a busy office.

### 2. Yoga

Yoga combines physical postures, breathwork, and meditation, making it an excellent tool for stress reduction and hormonal balance. Regular yoga practice has been shown to decrease cortisol levels, enhance mood, and improve overall physical health. Different styles of yoga, from gentle to more physically demanding types, can cater to individuals' varying fitness levels and stress-reduction needs.

### 3.Regular Exercise

Physical activity is a potent stress reliever. It helps release endorphins, natural mood elevators that can reduce stress and improve feelings of well-being. Additionally, exercise helps regulate all of the major hormones impacted by stress, including insulin and leptin. Activities can range from walking and cycling to more intense activities like interval training or sports.

### 4. Adequate Sleep

Sleep is crucial for hormonal balance. Lack of sleep can increase stress hormone levels and is linked to poor appetite regulation, diabetes, and heart disease. . Aiming for 7 to 9 hours of quality sleep per night is recommended for adults. Determining a regular sleep schedule, making the bedroom favorable to sleep, and avoiding caffeine and electronics before bed can improve sleep quality.

### 5. Balanced Diet

Eating a balanced diet not only helps manage weight but also supports hormonal health. Consuming foods that are high in omega-3 fatty acids, such as fish, flaxseeds, and walnuts, can help lower levels of the stress hormone cortisol and the adrenaline. Similarly, incorporating plenty of fruits, vegetables, whole grains, and lean proteins can help stabilize blood sugar and reduce stress.

### 6. Social Connections

Social interaction can help relieve stress. In addition to providing emotional support, enhancing emotions of belonging, and helping to lessen feelings of anxiety and depression, getting together with friends and family or engaging in activities in the community can be beneficial.

## Long-term Strategies for Hormonal Health

For long-term hormonal health and effective stress management, it is essential to adopt a holistic approach that includes lifestyle changes, dietary adjustments, and possibly professional support if stress becomes overwhelming.

Chronic stress is not only a risk factor for obesity and other metabolic issues but also for mental health disorders. Managing stress is thus not just about weight loss—it's about fostering a healthier, happier life.

Implementing these tactics into one's everyday activities can have a substantial impact on the quality of life achieved by the individual helping maintain hormonal balance, reducing stress, and promoting overall health and well-being. This holistic approach is what makes the GOLO diet effective not only as a weight loss tool but as a sustainable lifestyle change.

## Why the Golo Diet?

The Golo Diet stands apart from other diet plans because it's more than just a diet - it's a lifestyle transformation. It advocates for the joy of eating by promoting a diverse and balanced intake of nutrient-dense foods. The primary focus is on regulating insulin levels to support effective weight management and to maintain overall health, an essential aspect for both beginners and seniors.

This cookbook is your roadmap to incorporating the Golo Diet into your daily routine, with a bounty of delicious and recipes. It's designed to help you harness the advantages of the Golo Diet, such as improved energy levels, better control over blood sugar, and a more active and vibrant life.

## Why this Cookbook is an Essential Step?

Taking a new step in any diet can be an overwhelming process. Our cookbook takes out the hard leg work for you. In our cookbook, we understand exactly what foods will help regulate balanced insulin levels. For example, we opt for complex carbohydrates, such as quinoa and brown rice, which promote steady blood sugar levels. We prioritize lean protein sources like chicken, turkey, tofu, and legumes to support muscle health and satiety. When it comes to fats, we incorporate heart-healthy options like avocados, nuts, and olive oil in moderation.

We have designed this cookbook to limit your intake of added sugars and refined carbohydrates, as these can lead to blood sugar spikes. As you become familiar with the diet, you can save these recipes and become a master at managing your health. Always keep in mind that moderation, variety, and taking pleasure in the process of being healthier are the keys to success.

# CHAPTER 4
# Incorporating Physical Activity for Golo Benefits

Physical activity is a crucial component of the Golo lifestyle, playing a pivotal role in achieving and maintaining optimal health, weight management, and metabolic function. The Golo program emphasizes a balanced approach to nutrition and lifestyle, and regular exercise is a key element in supporting these goals. By incorporating physical activity into their daily routine, individuals can maximize the benefits of the Golo program, enhance metabolic health, and improve overall well-being.

## The Importance of Physical Activity

Participating in regular physical activity confers a wide variety of advantages that are congruent with the goals of the Golo program, including the following:

**Weight Management:** Engaging in regular exercise can support weight management by promoting calorie expenditure, enhancing metabolism, and contributing to the maintenance of lean muscle mass. This is particularly important for individuals seeking to achieve and sustain a healthy weight as part of the Golo lifestyle.

**Metabolic Health:** Physical activity plays a crucial role in improving insulin sensitivity, blood sugar regulation, and overall metabolic function. By incorporating regular exercise, individuals can support the goals of the Golo program to stabilize blood sugar levels and optimize metabolic health.

**Energy Expenditure:** Exercise contributes to increased energy expenditure, which can aid in creating a calorie deficit for weight loss and weight management. This is especially beneficial when combined with the balanced nutritional approach of the Golo program.

**Cardiovascular Health:** In addition to improving total cardiovascular function, regular physical activity can also improve cardiovascular health, lower the chance of developing chronic diseases including diabetes and heart disease, and improve overall cardiovascular function.

**Mental Well-Being:** : It has been demonstrated that physical activity has beneficial impacts on mental health, including the alleviation of stress, anxiety, and depression, as well as the enhancement of comprehensive well-being and cognitive performance.

## Strategies for Incorporating Physical Activity into the Golo Lifestyle

For individuals following the Golo lifestyle, there are several strategies that can help integrate physical activity into their daily routine to maximize the benefits of the program:

**Find Enjoyable Activities:** Choose physical activities that are enjoyable and sustainable. This could include walking, cycling, dancing, swimming, yoga, or any other form of exercise that aligns with individual preferences and interests.

**Set Realistic Goals:** Establish realistic goals for physical activity based on individual fitness levels, time availability, and personal preferences. Slowly elevate the duration and intensity of exercise as fitness improves.

**Consistency is Key:** Aim for consistency in physical activity by scheduling regular workouts or active pursuits throughout the week. Consistency is vital for reaping the long-term benefits of exercise.

**Variety:** Incorporate a variety of physical activities to engage different muscle groups, prevent boredom, and avoid overuse injuries. This can also contribute to overall fitness and functional strength.

**Functional Movement:** Focus on incorporating functional movements into daily activities to enhance overall fitness and support metabolic health. This could include activities such as gardening, housework, or taking the stairs instead of the elevator.

**Strength Training:** Comprise resistance training exercises to build muscle strength and support metabolic function. Resistance training can be performed using body weight, free weights, resistance bands, or other equipment.

**Supportive Environment:** Surround yourself with a supportive environment that encourages physical activity. This could involve finding a workout buddy, joining group fitness classes, or participating in community-based activities.

**Monitor Progress:** Keep track of physical activity progress by setting measurable goals and tracking workouts. This can provide motivation and accountability while allowing for adjustments based on individual needs and progress.

# CHAPTER 5
## Getting Started with the Golo Diet

Embarking on the GOLO journey is a transformative step toward better health, and it's essential to equip both beginners and seniors with practical tips and guidance to ensure a smooth and successful start. Whether you're new to the concept of insulin management or you're a senior looking to enhance your vitality, these tips will provide the support and encouragement needed to initiate your GOLO journey.

### For Beginners:

**Start Gradually:** Beginning any new dietary approach can be overwhelming. Start by incorporating small, manageable changes into your routine. This might involve swapping out sugary beverages for water or increasing your vegetable intake.

**Educate Yourself:** Take the time to learn about the principles of the GOLO diet and the role of insulin in weight management. Understanding the "why" behind the dietary changes can be motivating and empowering.

**Meal Planning:** You should think about making a meal plan in advance. This can assist you in making decisions that are conscious and avoiding choices that are less healthy and more impulsive. Begin with simple, balanced meals that align with the GOLO principles.

**Stay Hydrated:** Hydration is not only necessary for overall health but also has the potential to assist in the management of cravings. Make it a priority to consume a sufficient amount of water throughout the day.

**Seek Support:** Share your GOLO journey with friends or family members who can provide encouragement and accountability. Additionally, consider joining online communities or forums where you can connect with others on similar paths.

## For Seniors:

**Consult Your Healthcare Provider:** Before making any major alterations to your diet, it is recommended that you consult with your healthcare professional. This is particularly important if you are currently taking drugs or have any preexisting medical conditions. They have the ability to offer individualized advice that is tailored to your specific health profile.

**Focus on Nutrient Density:** As a senior, nutrient-dense foods are particularly important. These foods provide vital vitamins and minerals while often being lower in calories. Make sure that each of your meals has a wide range of colorful fruits and vegetables, lean meats, whole grains, and healthy fats.
**Mindful Eating:** Listen to the signals that your body sends you regarding hunger and fullness. Eating mindfully can serve as a means of preventing excessive eating and promoting healthy digestion.
**Regular Physical Activity:** Include participation in physical activity on a consistent basis in your regimen. Exercise not only supports overall health but also improves insulin sensitivity.

**Adapt Recipes:** Adjust recipes to meet your dietary preferences and any specific nutritional needs you may have. For example, if you need to limit sodium, look for ways to reduce salt in recipes without sacrificing flavor.

**Monitor Blood Sugar:** If you have diabetes or prediabetes, it's essential to monitor your blood sugar levels regularly. This can help you understand how different foods and meals affect your blood sugar and make informed choices. By offering these tailored tips for both beginners and seniors, we aim to ensure that everyone embarking on their GOLO journey does so with confidence and success. These tips are not just practical; they are empowering, emphasizing that the path to better health is achievable through gradual, sustainable changes.

## Getting a Grip on Nutrition Basics

Maintaining a balanced diet forms the foundation for health. It entails consuming the amounts and proportions of nutrients that your body requires. Let's delve into these nutrients:

## Macronutrients

**Carbohydrates:** misunderstood and unfairly criticized carbohydrates are vital for fueling your energy levels. They break down into glucose, which serves as the source of energy for both your brain and muscles. Complex carbohydrates found in grains and vegetables offer a release of energy keeping you satisfied and full for longer durations.

**Proteins:** Crucial for tissue repair and building proteins act as the building blocks for muscles organs, enzymes and hormones. Meats, fish, and dairy products, in addition to plant-based options such as lentils and tofu, are all noteworthy examples of great sources of high-quality protein.

**Fats:** Fats play a role in vitamin absorption and organ protection. They serve as sources of energy while also contributing to hormone production. Healthy fats present in foods such, as avocados, nuts and olive oil should be incorporated into your diet.

## Micronutrients

Micronutrients refer to vitamins and minerals that're necessary for various bodily functions. For example, calcium and vitamin D are crucial, for maintaining bones iron supports blood production and vitamin C helps boost function. A diverse diet that includes fruits, vegetables, whole grains, lean proteins and healthy fats ensures an intake of these micronutrients.

Fiber and Hydration: Fiber plays a role in managing weight and promoting health. Both your blood sugar levels and your feeling of fullness are stabilized as a result of this. Hydration is equally vital as it aids in digestion regulates body temperature and supports functions. In the Golo Diet emphasis is placed on consuming fiber and staying hydrated to support your goals as well as overall wellbeing. A balanced diet promotes health by sustaining energy levels supporting organ function and bolstering the system. It's not about managing weight; it's about nurturing your body at a level. Each nutrient has its contribution to weight management:

**Complex Carbohydrates:** These provide a consistent release of energy. When you consume carbs they gradually elevate your blood sugar levels without causing spikes, in insulin production. This helps reduce storage while keeping you satiated for durations, ultimately aiding in weight control.

**Lean Proteins:** Proteins have an effect, on metabolism. They require energy to digest, absorb and assimilate compared to fats and carbs. This leads to an increase in metabolic rate. Moreover, proteins play a role in muscle repair and growth which's important because muscles burn more calories than fat even when at rest.

**Healthy Fats:** Despite being high in calories fats are essential for managing weight. They contribute to the feeling of fullness. Assist in the regulation of hunger hormones, making it possible to consume fewer calories. Additionally, fats are necessary for the absorption of vitamins (A D, E and K) which have various functions in maintaining a healthy metabolism.

Your metabolism encompasses all the chemical processes that convert food into energy. Let's explore how different nutrients impact your metabolism:

**Carbohydrates:** These are the bodys energy source. Once digested carbs are converted into glucose. Used immediately for energy or stored as glycogen in muscles and the liver for use. The body efficiently metabolizes carbohydrates, ones, which provides a steady supply of energy.

**Proteins:** Metabolizing protein requires energy, from the body compared to carbs and fats. The phenomenon known as the effect of food (TEF) comes into play here. Protein in particular contributes to an increase, in metabolic rate after a meal. Helps maintain muscle mass, which is important for keeping your metabolism high.

**Fats:** Fats are broken down slowly. Provide a steady source of energy. The process of breaking down fats involves converting triglycerides into glycerol and free fatty acids through lipolysis. While fats have a thermic effect compared to proteins they play a role in maintaining overall energy balance and aiding nutrient absorption.

Understanding these aspects of nutrition is essential as you begin the Golo Diet. A rounded intake of carbohydrates, proteins and fats along with vitamins and minerals forms the basis for successful weight management and overall wellbeing. As you progress through the Golo Diet journey this knowledge will empower you to make choices about the foods that align with your health goals.

## Integrating Dietary Supplements with the GOLO Diet

While the GOLO diet is designed to be comprehensive, providing a wide array of nutrients through a balanced diet, there are instances where incorporating dietary supplements can enhance overall health outcomes, particularly in achieving hormonal balance and enhancing metabolic functions.

This section explores how dietary supplements can complement the GOLO diet and how to safely integrate them into your daily routine.

## The Value of Supplements in a Balanced Diet

Even the most meticulously planned diets can fall short in providing all essential nutrients. Factors such as the quality of soil where the food was grown, the storage and transportation of food items, and individual health conditions can lead to nutritional gaps. Supplements can play a crucial role in filling these gaps, ensuring that the body receives all the nutrients it needs for optimal function.

For those on the GOLO diet aiming to manage weight and enhance metabolic health, supplements like omega-3 fatty acids can be particularly beneficial. These essential fats are crucial for reducing inflammation and supporting brain health, which in turn can aid in weight management and improve metabolic processes.

Similarly, probiotics can help maintain a healthy gut flora, essential for effective digestion and absorption of nutrients, while also playing a role in regulating metabolic hormones such as insulin and leptin.

## Critical Supplements to Consider

**Multivitamins**: These provide a broad spectrum of vitamins and minerals, acting as a safety net to ensure you're getting a sufficient amount of essential nutrients daily.

**Omega-3 Fatty Acids**: Important for assisting in the maintenance of neurological health and decreasing inflammation, which is crucial for managing body weight and hormonal balance.

**Magnesium**: This mineral is involved in numerous biochemical reactions in the body, including those regulating blood sugar and blood pressure, and is also important for sleep and muscle function.

**Vitamin D**: Crucial for immune function, bone health, and muscle function, vitamin D also aids in the absorption of calcium and has a role in neuromuscular and immune function.

**B-Complex Vitamins**: Essential for energy production and metabolic processes, these vitamins help the body utilize fats and proteins effectively and are crucial for maintaining healthy skin, hair, and eyes.

**Fiber Supplements**: Useful for enhancing satiety, managing blood sugar levels, and supporting digestive health, especially when dietary intake is lacking.

**Adaptogens like Ashwagandha**: These can help the body manage stress more effectively, supporting adrenal health and overall hormone balance.

## Safely Adding Supplements to Your Diet

Before incorporating any supplements into your diet, it is imperative that you discuss the matter with a healthcare expert. This is particularly important if you are already taking prescription medications or have any pre-existing health conditions. This step is crucial to ensure there are no adverse interactions with any medications you're currently taking and to tailor supplement recommendations to your specific health needs.

When choosing supplements, opt for high-quality brands that independently test their products for purity and potency. Starting with a lower dose and gradually increasing to the recommended level can help minimize any potential side effects and allow you to monitor how your body responds to the supplement.

It's also important to stay vigilant about how you integrate supplements into your diet. Some supplements can interact with each other or with prescription medications, potentially leading to adverse effects. For example, high doses of magnesium can interfere with certain antibiotics, and omega-3 supplements can increase bleeding risk, particularly if you are on blood thinners.

Regularly revisiting your supplement strategy is also wise, as your nutritional needs may change over time due to aging, health changes, or lifestyle adjustments. Regular check-ins with your healthcare provider can help adjust your supplement intake based on your current health status and goals.

While supplements should not replace a balanced diet, they can certainly enhance the nutritional completeness of the GOLO diet. With careful consideration and professional guidance, the right supplements can support your dietary efforts, enhance your overall health, and contribute to a more balanced hormonal profile, all of which are integral to achieving sustainable health improvements.

# CHAPTER 6
## Adapting the GOLO Diet for Different Life Stages

The nutritional needs of an individual can vary significantly throughout their life due to changes in metabolism, activity levels, and specific health requirements. Understanding these changes is crucial for adapting dietary approaches such as the GOLO diet to meet the unique needs of different age groups. This section will explore how the GOLO diet can be tailored for adolescents, adults, and seniors, providing modifications to recipes, essential nutrient integrations, and advice for addressing common age-related concerns.

### Nutrition for Adolescents

During adolescence, the body undergoes significant growth and development, which increases the demand for energy and nutrients. For teenagers, a modified GOLO diet needs to support these rapid physical changes without compromising the hormonal balance and energy levels that are crucial during these formative years.

### Key Nutritional Focus Areas:

**Increased Protein**: Adolescents require more protein to help with muscle and tissue development. Incorporating lean proteins such as chicken, turkey, fish, and plant-based proteins like beans and lentils can ensure they are meeting their growth needs.

**Calcium and Vitamin D**: Essential for bone development, adequate calcium intake paired with vitamin D is critical during the teenage years. Dairy products fortified with vitamin D, leafy greens, and calcium-set tofu are excellent sources.

**Iron**: Particularly important for girls who begin menstruation, iron helps prevent anemia. Iron-rich foods like red meat, spinach, and iron-fortified cereals should be emphasized.

## Dietary Modifications:

Include more snack options that are rich in nutrients, such as yogurt with nuts and fruit, or smoothies made with spinach and berries to attract younger palates while providing essential nutrients.

Ensure meals are adaptable to a teenager's active lifestyle, with portable options that can be packed for school lunches or quick dinners.

## Nutrition for Adults

As adults, the focus shifts to maintaining optimal health, managing weight, and preventing lifestyle diseases such as diabetes and hypertension. The metabolic rate starts to slow down, making it essential to adapt the GOLO diet to prevent weight gain and support energy levels throughout the day.

## Key Nutritional Focus Areas:

**Balanced Macronutrients**: It's crucial to balance carbohydrates, proteins, and fats to maintain energy levels and metabolic health. Focus on whole grains, lean proteins, and healthy fats from oils, nuts, and seeds.

**Fiber**: Fiber is beneficial to digestion and assists in the maintenance of a healthy weight. Adults should aim for a mix of soluble and insoluble fiber from vegetables, fruits, legumes, and whole grains.

**Antioxidants**: Combat oxidative stress with foods rich in antioxidants like berries, nuts, and dark chocolate, which also help prevent chronic diseases.

## Dietary Modifications:

Prepare meals that are easy to digest and nutrient-dense, such as grilled salmon with quinoa and steamed vegetables, to cater to a slowing metabolism.

Incorporate foods that support heart health and reduce cholesterol, such as oats and avocado.

## Nutrition for Seniors

For seniors, nutritional needs shift towards sustaining health, preserving cognitive function, and managing chronic health issues. Decreased activity levels and metabolic rate mean the GOLO diet should focus on nutrient density over caloric intake to prevent muscle loss and bone density reduction.

## Key Nutritional Focus Areas:

**Protein**: Essential for preserving muscle mass, which declines with age. Opt for easily digestible protein sources like fish, poultry, and whey protein.

**Calcium and Vitamin D**: Continued focus on these nutrients helps combat the risk of osteoporosis. Supplements might be necessary based on individual health assessments.

**B Vitamins**: Particularly vitamin B12, which might be harder to absorb with age and is crucial for cognitive function.

## Dietary Modifications:

Adapt recipes to be softer and easier to chew, such as using slow-cooked meats and softer vegetables, which can also help with digestion. Create meals that are easy to prepare, acknowledging that seniors might have decreased energy for complex meal preparation. Adapting the GOLO diet to accommodate different stages of life ensures that each individual can meet their specific nutritional needs and manage health concerns effectively. By modifying recipes, focusing on essential nutrients, and offering practical dietary advice for common issues at each life stage, the GOLO diet can support a healthy lifestyle from adolescence through to senior years. This comprehensive approach not only enhances physical health but also contributes to overall well-being and quality of life across the lifespan.

INIZIO MODULO

# Breakfast

## Protein-Packed Omelette

**Ingredients:**
- 2 big eggs
- ¼ cup diced bell peppers
- ¼ cup diced onions
- ¼ cup diced tomatoes
- ¼ cup chopped spinach
- Salt and pepper as required

**Directions:**
1. In a bowl, blend the eggs, salt, and pepper by whisking them together.
2. Put a splash of olive oil in a skillet that does not adhere to the pan and heat it at a middling temp.
3. In the meantime, pour the egg mixture into the skillet and allow it to cook for 2 to 3 minutes, or until the edges begin to solidify. Over the eggs, distribute the diced vegetables in an equal layer.
4. To fold the omelette in half, use a spatula, and continue cooking it for additional 2 to 3 minutes, or until the eggs have reached their full set.
5. Slide the omelette onto a plate and serve hot.

**Nutrition:**

*Calories: 220  Protein: 18g  Fat: 12g  Carbs: 10g  Fiber: 3g*

## Quinoa Breakfast Bowl

**Ingredients:**
- 1/2 cup quinoa, washed
- 1 cup water or unsweetened almond milk
- 1/2 tsp cinnamon
- 1/4 cup sliced almonds
- 1/2 cup mixed berries (strawberries, blueberries, raspberries)
- 1 tbsp honey or maple syrup (optional)

**Directions:**
1. In a saucepan, blend quinoa, water or almond milk, and cinnamon.
2. Bring to a boil, then put a lid on the pot, decrease the temp. to low, and continue to simmer for 12 to 15 minutes, or until the quinoa is cooked and the liquid has passed through.
3. The third step is to use a fork to fluff the quinoa and then divide it into two dishes. Top each bowl with sliced almonds, mixed berries, and a drizzle of honey or maple syrup (if using).
4. Top each bowl with sliced almonds, mixed berries, and a drizzle of honey or maple syrup (if using).
5. Present warm and enjoy!

**Nutrition:**

*Calories: 320  Protein: 10g  Fat: 10g  Carbs: 50g  Fiber: 8g*

## Banana Nut Overnight Oats

### Ingredients:

- 1/2 cup rolled oats
- 1/2 cup unsweetened almond milk
- 1/2 ripe banana, mashed
- 1 tbsp chopped walnuts
- 1 tbsp honey or maple syrup (optional)

### Directions:

1. In a mason jar or sealed container, combine rolled oats, almond milk, mashed banana, chopped walnuts, and honey or maple syrup (if using).
2. Blend thoroughly by stirring.
3. Cover the jar and place it in the fridge for the night.
4. After giving the oats a thorough stir in the morning, you may either eat them cold or warm.

### Nutrition

*Calories: 280 Protein: 8g Fat: 10g Carbs: 40g Fiber: 6g*

# Veggie Breakfast Burrito

## Ingredients:

- 2 whole grain tortillas
- 1/2 cup black beans, drained and washed
- 1/2 cup diced bell peppers
- 1/4 cup diced onions
- 1/4 cup shredded cheddar cheese
- 2 eggs, beaten
- Salt and pepper as required

## Directions:

1. Warma non-stick skillet at middling temp. and spray with cooking spray.
2. In a skillet, include the diced onions and bell peppers, and sauté them for around 3 to 4 minutes, or until they have become more tender.
3. Put the black beans in the skillet and continue to cook them for another 2-3 minutes, until they are completely heated through.
4. Once the veggie combination has been pushed to one side of the skillet, pour the eggs that have been beaten into the other side of the skillet.
5. Cook the eggs, stirring occasionally, until scrambled and cooked through.
6. Divide the egg mixture, vegetable mixture, and shredded cheese evenly between the tortillas.
7. In order to make burritos, roll the tortillas up and fold the sides in as you press them together.
8. Put the burritos on the skillet with the seam side down and cook them for 2 to 3 minutes on all sides, until they are golden brown and crispy. Place the burritos seam side down in the skillet and cook for 2-3 minutes on each side until golden brown and crispy.
9. Present hot with salsa or hot sauce if desired.

**Nutrition:**

*Calories: 350 Protein: 18g Fat: 14g Carbs: 40g Fiber:10g*

# Overnight Oats with Berries

## Ingredients:

- 1/3 cup of rolled oats
- ½ cup of unsweetened almond milk
- ½ cup of mixed berries (fresh or frozen)
- 1 tsp of chia seeds
- 1 tbsp of honey or maple syrup (optional)

## Directions:

1. In a mason jar or bowl, combine the oats, almond milk, and chia seeds.
2. Stir until well combined, and then add the mixed berries on top.
3. Cover the jar or bowl, and put in the fridge overnight.
4. Do a thorough mixing of the oats first thing in the morning.
5. Honey or maple syrup can be used to sweeten the mixture, and then it can be enjoyed

**Nutrition:**

*Calories: 225 Protein: 7g Fat: 5g Carbs: 40g Fiber: 9g*

## EGG AND VEGGIE SCRAMBLE

### INGREDIENTS:
- 2 big egg
- 1 cup of mixed vegetables (like bell peppers, onions, and spinach)
- 1 tbsp of olive oil
- Salt and pepper as required

### DIRECTIONS:
1. In a skillet that does not stick, bring the olive oil to a middling temp.
2. After adding the vegetables, sauté them until they acquire a tender consistency. Put the eggs in another bowl and beat them. Over the vegetables that are already in the skillet, pour them.
3. Stir the eggs carefully until they are completely cooked through.
4. Season to taste with your choice of salt and pepper, and then present.

**Nutrition:**

*Calories: 250 Protein: 12g Fat: 18g Carbs: 10g Fiber: 3g*

# Chia Pudding with Fruit

## Ingredients:
- 2 tbsp of chia seeds
- ½ cup of unsweetened almond milk
- ½ cup of mixed fresh fruits (like berries, kiwi, and mango)
- 1 tbsp of honey or maple syrup (optional)

## Directions:
1. In a mason jar or bowl, mix the chia seeds and almond milk.
2. Stir until well combined, cover, and put in the fridge for almost 4 hours or overnight until it becomes a pudding-like consistency.
3. Top with fresh fruits and drizzle with honey or maple syrup if desired before serving.

**Nutrition:**

Calories: 225 Protein: 6g Fat: 11g Carbs: 25g Fiber: 10g

# Avocado Toast on Whole Grain Bread

## Ingredients
- 1 slice of whole grain bread
- ½ ripe avocado
- A pinch of salt
- A pinch of black pepper
- ½ tsp of lemon juice
- Optional toppings:
- chia seeds, sesame seeds, or red pepper flakes for added flavor and nutrients.

## Directions:
1. Toasted bread is made with whole grains until it reaches a golden brown colour.
2. Put the ripe avocado in a bowl and mash it. Put in the lemon juice, and season it with salt and pepper according to preference.
3. On the bread that has been toasted, spread the mashed avocado in a uniform layer.
4. If desired, sprinkle with your choice of topping.
5. Present immediately for a fresh and healthy breakfast or snack.

**Nutrition:**

Calories 235, protein 7g, fat 15g, carbs 23g, fiber 10g

# Spinach and Feta Frittata

## Ingredients

- 2bigt eggs
- ½ cup of fresh spinach, roughly chopped
- ¼ cup of feta cheese, crumbled
- Salt and pepper as required
- ½ tbsp on of olive oil

## Directions:

1. Warm up your oven to 375 deg.F (190 deg.C).
2. In a bowl, beat the eggs using a whisk. Spinach, feta cheese, salt, and pepper should be added to the dish, after thoroughly combining, mix.
3. Put the olive oil in a skillet that can go in the oven and heat it at a middling temp.
4. When you pour the egg mixture into the skillet, make sure that the spinach and feta are distributed equally throughout the mixture.
5. Cook for a couple of minutes, or until the edges begin to pull away from the skillet, whichever comes first. After the oven has been prepared, place the skillet inside and bake for around 10 to 12 minutes, or until the frittata has thickened in the centre.
6. Before cutting into the frittata, wait a couple of minutes for it to cool down and then proceed to cut it. I would recommend serving it warm with a side of toast made with natural grains.

**Nutrition**

*calories 320, protein 20g, fat 25g, carbs 5g, fiber 1g*

# Healthy Banana Pancakes

## Ingredients

- 1 ripe banana
- 2 big eggs
- A pinch of cinnamon
- ½ tbsp of olive oil or butter for cooking

## Directions:

1. In a bowl, mash the ripe banana until it's free of big lumps.
2. Whisk in the eggs and a pinch of cinnamon until well combined.
3. The next step is to heat the butter or olive oil in a skillet that does not stick at middling temp.
4. Transfer the batter to the skillet and use it to make 2 to 3 separate pancakes.
5. Give them a golden brown colour by cooking them for approximately 2 to 3 minutes on all sides.
6. If wanted, serve the dish warm with a drizzle of honey or a sprinkling of additional cinnamon.

**Nutrition**

*calories 270, protein 14g, fat 13g, carbs 27g, fiber 3g*

# Sweet Potato Hash

## Ingredients:

- 1 big sweet potato, diced
- ½ cup diced bell peppers
- ¼ cup diced onions
- ¼ cup diced tomatoes
- Salt and pepper as required

## Directions:

1. Spray a non-stick skillet with cooking spray and heat it at a middling temp. when it is available.
2. Put the sweet potato that has been diced into the skillet and cook it for 10 to 12 minutes, tossing it irregularly, until it is soft and has received a light brown colour.
3. After the bell peppers, onions, and tomatoes have been diced, add them to the skillet and continue to simmer for an extra 5 to 7 minutes, until the vegetables have become smaller.
4. The fourth step is to move the vegetable combination to one side of the skillet and then crack the eggs into the other side of the skillet.
5. After the eggs have been cooked to the degree of doneness that you choose, season them with salt and pepper.
6. Present the sweet potato hash topped with the cooked eggs.

**Nutrition**

*Calories: 350 Protein: 15g Fat: 10g Carbs: 50g Fiber: 8g*

# Almond Milk and Oats Porridge

## Ingredients
- 1/2 cup of rolled oats
- 1 cup of unsweetened almond milk
- 1 tbsp of honey or maple syrup
- A handful of your favorite berries

## Directions:
1. First, put the rolled oats and almond milk into a pot and mix them together.
2. To begin, bring the ingredients to a boil, and then decrease the temp. to a simmer.
3. Cook the oats, stirring occasionally, for around 10-15 minutes or until the oats are your desired level of creaminess.
4. Stir in the honey or maple syrup.
5. Put the oats in a bowl and choose the berries that you like best to top them with.
6. present warm, ideally for a heart-warming breakfast on a cold morning.

**Nutrition**

*calories 285, protein 9g, fat 8g, carbs 45g, fiber 8g*

# Lunch

## Quinoa and Black Bean Stuffed Peppers

**Ingredients:**

- 4 bell peppers, divided and seedstaken out.
- 1 cup quinoa, cooked
- 1 can (15 oz) black beans, washedand drained
- 1 cup corn kernels
- ½ cup diced tomatoes
- ½ cup diced red onion
- ¼ cup chopped fresh cilantro
- 1 tsp cumin
- ½ tsp chili powder
- Salt and pepper as required
- ½ cup shredded cheddar cheese (optional)

**Directions:**

1. Warm up the oven to 375 deg.F (190 deg.C).
2. Blend the quinoa that has been cooked, the black beans, the corn, the diced tomatoes, the red onion, the cilantro, the cumin, the chilli powder, the salt, and the pepper in a big container.
3. The third step is to stuff each side of the bell pepper with the quinoa mixture and then set them on a baking dish. Sprinkle shredded cheddar cheese on top of the peppers that have been filled, if you are using it.
4. In a baking dish, cover it with aluminium foil and bake it for 25 to 30 minutes, or until the peppers are soft.

**Nutrition**

*Calories: 280 Protein: 12g Fat: 4g Carbs: 50g Fiber: 10g*

## Tuna Salad Stuffed Bell Peppers

**Ingredients:**

- 4 bell peppers, divided and seeds taken out
- 2 cans (5 oz each) tuna, drained
- 1/4 cup Greek yogurt
- 2 tbsps lemon juice
- 1/4 cup diced celery
- 1/4 cup diced red onion
- 1/4 cup diced cucumber
- 2 tbsps chopped fresh parsley
- Salt and pepper as required

**Directions:**

1. In a big mixing bowl, blend drained tuna, Greek yogurt, lemon juice, diced celery, diced red onion, diced cucumber, chopped fresh parsley, salt, and pepper.
2. The mixture should be thoroughly mixed and creamy.
3. Spoon tuna salad mixture into each bell pepper half, filling them evenly.
4. As an option for a meal that is both light and refreshing, present instantly.

**Nutrition**

*Calories: 220 Protein: 25g Fat: 8g Carbs: 15g Fiber: 5*

# Black Bean and Corn Quesadillas

## Ingredients:

- 4 whole wheat tortillas
- 1 can (15 oz) black beans, washed and drained
- 1 cup corn kernels
- 1/2 cup diced tomatoes
- 1/4 cup diced red onion
- 1/2 cup shredded cheddar cheese
- 1/4 cup chopped fresh cilantro
- Cooking spray
- Optional toppings:
- sliced avocado, Greek yogurt, salsa

## Directions:

1. Blend black beans, corn kernels, diced tomatoes, diced red onion, shredded cheddar cheese, and chopped cilantro in a big mixing bowl.
2. Arrange the tortillas made from whole wheat flat on a surface that is level.
3. Distribute the black bean mixture across one-half of each tortilla in a uniform manner.
4. Create a half-moon shape by folding the other half of the tortilla over the filling to form a semicircle.
5. Warm a non-stick skillet at a middling temp. and immediately spray it with cooking spray in a light coating.
6. Transfer the quesadillas to the skillet in a careful manner and cook them for two to three minutes on each side, or until they are deep golden brown and crispy.
7. When you are ready to cut the meat into wedges, take it out from the skillet and allow it to cool for a minute.
8. If preferred, serve hot with one or more toppings of your choice.

### Nutrition

*Calories: 280 Protein: 15g Fat: 10g Carbs: 35g Fiber: 8g*

# Mushroom Barley Soup

## Ingredients:

- 1 tbsp olive oil
- 1 onion, diced
- 2 carrots, diced
- 2 celery stalks, diced
- 8 oz mushrooms, cut
- 2 pieces garlic, crushed
- 1 cup pearl barley
- 6 cups vegetable broth
- 1 tsp dried thyme
- Salt and pepper as required
- Fresh parsley, chopped
- (for garnish)

## Directions:

1. Bring the olive oil to a simmer in a big saucepan at a middling temp.
2. Include diced onion, carrots, and celery, and continue to cook for approximately 5 minutes, or until the vegetables have become more tender.
3. To the pot, include sliced mushrooms and garlic that have been minced, and continue to cook for a further 5 minutes, or until the mushrooms have reached a golden brown colour.
4. Put the pearl barley, vegetable broth, dried thyme, salt, and pepper into a bowl and stir to combine.
5. After bringing the soup to a boil, decrease the temp. to a low setting and continue to simmer for 30 to 40 minutes, or until the barley is soft and the soup has thickened.
6. Adjust the spice to your liking, and serve the dish hot, garnished with fresh parsley that has been chopped.

### Nutrition:

*Calories: 250 Protein: 8g Fat: 4g Carbs: 45g Fiber: 10g*

# Chicken and Avocado Wrap

## Ingredients

- 1 small chicken breast
- ½ ripe avocado, cut
- 1 whole grain wrap or tortilla
- A handful of mixed salad greens
- 1/4 tomato, cut
- 1 tbsp of Greek yogurt
- Salt and pepper as required

## Directions:

1. Season the chicken breast with salt and pepper. Grill or pan-fry until fully cooked, then allow it to relax for a couple of minutes prior to cutting
2. Lay the whole grain wrap on a flat surface. Spread the Greek yogurt down the center. Top with the salad greens, tomato slices, avocado slices, and sliced chicken.
3. Take the wrap and roll it up, making sure to tuck in the sides as you go.
4. present chilled or at room temperature. This wrap is a balanced, portable meal that's perfect for lunch on the go.

### Nutrition

*calories 420, protein 30g, fat 20g, carbs 30g, fiber 10g*

# Turkey Chili with Beans

## Ingredients:

- 1 tbsp olive oil
- 1 onion, diced
- 2 picese garlic, crushed
- 1-pound lean ground turkey
- 1 can (15 oz) black beans, washed and drained
- 1 can (15 oz.) kidney beans, washed and drained
- 1 can (14.5 oz.) diced tomatoes
- 1 cup tomato sauce
- 1 cup chicken broth
- 1 tbsp[ chili powder
- 1 tsp cumin
- ½ tsp paprika
- Salt and pepper as required
- Optional toppings:
- Shredded cheese, diced
- Avocado
- Greek yogurt
- Chopped cilantro

## Directions:

1. Bring the olive oil to a simmer in a big saucepan at a middling temp. Within 5 minutes after adding the crushed garlic and diced onion, the onion should have become more tender.
2. Put the ground turkey in the pot, using a spoon to break it up, and continue to cook it until it starts to brown.
3. Stir in black beans, kidney beans, diced tomatoes, tomato sauce, chicken broth, chili powder, cumin, paprika, salt, and pepper.
4. When the chilli reaches a boil, decrease the temp. to a low setting and continue to simmer for thirty to forty minutes while mixing it intermittently.
5. Adjust seasoning as required and serve hot with optional toppings, if desired.

**Nutrition**

*Calories: 300 Protein: 25g Fat: 8g Carbs: 30g Fiber: 10g*

## GRILLED CHICKEN SALAD WITH BALSAMIC VINAIGRETTE

### INGREDIENTS:

- 2 boneless, skinless chicken breasts
- 6 cups mixed greens
- 1 cup cherry tomatoes, divided
- 1 cucumber, cut
- ¼ red onion, finely cut
- ¼ cup crumbled feta cheese
- ¼ cup balsamic vinegar
- 2 tbsps extra virgin olive oil
- Salt and pepper as required

### DIRECTIONS:

1. Bring the grill up to a medium-high temp.
2. Include salt and pepper in chicken breasts and season their meat. For chicken, grill it for 6-7 minutes on all sides, or until it is completely cooked through.
3. In a small bowl, whisk together balsamic vinegar and olive oil to make the vinaigrette.
4. Put the mixed greens, cherry tomatoes, cucumber, red onion, and feta cheese in a big salad bowl until everything is evenly distributed.
5. After grilling the chicken, slice it and lay it on top of the salad.
6. Drizzle with balsamic vinaigrette and toss to coat.

**Nutrition**

*Calories: 320 Protein: 30g Fat: 15g Carbs: 10g Fiber: 4g*

# Veggie and Hummus Sandwich

## Ingredients
- 2 slices of whole grain bread
- 2 tbsps of hummus
- A handful of mixed salad greens
- 1/4 cucumber, cut
- 1/4 bell pepper, cut
- 1/4 tomato, cut
- Salt and pepper as required

## Directions:
1. A single slice of bread should be used to spread the hummus on it.
2. Top with the salad greens, cucumber slices, bell pepper slices, and tomato slices. Sprinkle with salt and pepper.
3. Position the second slice of bread on top of the first.
4. Present cold or at room temp., whatever you choose. This sandwich is a snack that is not only light but also nutritional, as it is loaded with vegetables and fiber.

### Nutrition

*calories 320, protein 12g, fat 10g, carbs 45g, fiber 10g*

# Stuffed Bell Peppers

## Ingredients

- 1 bell pepper
- 1/4 cup of cooked quinoa
- 1/4 cup of canned black beans, drained and washed
- 1/4 cup of corn kernels
- 1/4 onion, diced
- 1/4 cup of shredded cheddar cheese
- 1 tbsp of olive oil
- Salt and pepperas required

## Directions:

1. Warm up your oven to 375 deg.F (190 deg.C). The top of the bell pepper should be cut off, and the seeds should be removed. Put it away for later.
2. Warm the olive oil in a saucepan at a middling temp. Sauté the onion until it has attained a mellow state.
3. To the pan, include the quinoa that has been cooked, the black beans, and the corn. Mix everything together and bring it to a boil.
4. To fill the bell pepper, spoon the quinoa mixture inside the pepper. Using the shredded cheese, top the dish.
5. The filled bell pepper should be placed in a baking dish and baked for approximately 20 minutes, or until the pepper is soft and the cheese has melted throughout the pepper.
6. present hot, with a side salad or steamed veggies if desired.

### Nutrition

*calories 390, protein 15g, fat 15g, carbs 45g, fiber 10g*

# Spinach and Tomato Stuffed Chicken

## Ingredients

- 1 small chicken breast
- ¼ cup of fresh spinach leaves
- ¼ tomato, cut
- ¼ cup of shredded mozzarella cheese
- ½ tbsp of olive oil
- Salt and pepper as required .

## Directions:

1. Warm up your oven to 375deg F (190 deg C).
2. Cut a pocket into the side of the chicken breast. Take extra precautions to avoid cutting all the way through.
3. Stuff the pocket with the spinach leaves, tomato slices, and mozzarella cheese.
4. Rub the chicken with the olive oil, then sprinkle with salt and pepper.
5. Put the chicken on a baking sheet and bake for about 25-30 minutes, or until fully cooked.
6. Present hot with a side of steamed veggies or a mixed green salad.

### Nutrition

*calories 280, protein 30g, fat 14g, carbs 4g, fiber 1g*

# Sweet Potato and Black Bean Chili

## Ingredients

- 1 small sweet potato, skinned and diced
- ½ cup of canned black beans, drained and washed
- ½ cup of vegetable broth
- ¼ onion, diced
- ¼ bell pepper, diced
- 1 garlic piece, crushed
- A dash of chili powder
- 1 tbsp of olive oil
- Salt and pepper as required

## Directions:

1. First, bring the olive oil to a simmer in a saucepan at a middling temp. The onion, bell pepper, and garlic should be sautéed until they have become more tender.
2. Secondly, include the sweet potato, black beans, broth, chilli powder, salt, and pepper into the mixture. Allow to come to a simmer.
3. Put the lid on the saucepan and cook for approximately 20 minutes, or until the sweet potato is cooked.
4. If you so want, serve the dish while it is still hot, with a dollop of Greek yoghurt and a sprinkling of shredded cheddar cheese to garnish.

### Nutrition

*calories 350, protein 10g, fat 10g, carbs 60g, fiber 10g*

# Veggie and Brown Rice Stir Fry

## Ingredients

- 1/2 cup of cooked brown rice
- 1/4 bell pepper, cut
- 1/4 onion, sliced
- 1/4 zucchini, cut
- 1/2 carrot, cut
- 1/2 tbsp of low-sodium soy sauce
- 1/2 tbsp of olive oil
- Salt and pepper as required.

## Directions:

1. Bring the olive oil to a simmer in a big frying pan or wok that is set at a middling temp. While the carrot, zucchini, onion, and bell pepper are being sautéed, the bell pepper should be added.
2. Include the rice that has been cooked and the soy sauce, and mix until everything is thoroughly incorporated and heated through. Include salt and pepper as required and season with salt.
3. present hot, topped with a sprinkle of sesame seeds or a drizzle of sriracha for a bit of a kick, if desired.

**Nutrition**

*calories 240, protein 5g, fat 7g, carbs 40g, fiber 5g*

# Dinner

## GRILLED BEEF KEBABS WITH VEGETABLES

**INGREDIENTS:**

- 1-lb beef sirloin, cut into 1" cubes
- 1 bell pepper, cut into chunks
- 1 red onion, cut into chunks
- 8 cherry tomatoes
- For Marinade:
- 1/4 cup olive oil
- 2 tbsps soy sauce
- 2 pieces garlic, minced
- 1 tsp paprika
- 1 tsp ground cumin
- 1 tsp dried oregano
- Salt and pepper as required.
- Wooden skewers, soaked in water for 30 minutes

**DIRECTIONS:**

1. To prepare the marinade, combine the following ingredients in a bowl: olive oil, soy sauce, minced garlic, paprika, ground cumin, dried oregano, salt, and pepper. Whisk until well combined.
2. Toss the meat cubes in the marinade until they are equally coated with the marinade, after allowing them to marinade for almost half an hour.
3. Thread the beef cubes that have been marinated, the bell pepper chunks, the red onion chunks, and the cherry tomatoes onto wooden skewers that have been soaked.
4. Bring your grill up to a medium-high temp.
5. Put the kebabs on the grill and cook them for a few minutes on all sides, or until the meat is cooked to the degree of doneness that you choose and the vegetables are soft.
6. After removing the food from the grill, provide it with a couple of minutes of rest prior to presenting.

**Nutrition:**

*calories: 320 proteins: 25g fat: 20g carbs: 8g fiber:2g*

# CAULIFLOWER FRIED RICE WITH TOFU

## INGREDIENTS:

- 1 head cauliflower, riced
- 1 block extra-firm tofu, pressed and cubed
- Mixed vegetables (such as peas, carrots, and onions)
- Soy sauce or tamari
- Sesame oil
- Scrambled eggs (optional)

## DIRECTIONS:

1. In a big skillet, bring the sesame oil to a middling temp.
2. Include the cubes of tofu and fry them until they are golden brown on all sides. After removing from the skillet, put it away.
3. Include a variety of veggies in the same skillet and sauté them until they are soft.
4. Stir in cauliflower rice and cooked tofu, then drizzle with soy sauce or tamari as required.
5. If desired, add scrambled eggs and continue to cook until heated through.

**Nutrition**

Calorie: 400, Protein: 30g, Fat: 15g, Carb: 30g

# BAKED LEMON HERB CHICKEN WITH QUINOA

## INGREDIENTS

- 4 bonoless, skinless chicken breasts
- 1 cup quinoa
- 1 lemon (sliced)
- 4 pieces garlic (curshed)
- 2 cups fresh spinach
- 2 tbsps olive oil
- Salt and pepper as required.

## DIRECTIONS

1. Warm upthe oven to 400 degF (200 degC).
2. Season chicken breasts with salt, pepper, and crushed garlic. Could you put them in a baking dish?
3. Surround the chicken with quinoa, fresh spinach, and lemon slices.
4. Drizzle olive oil over the ingredients.
5. Bake for 25 minutes or until the chicken is cooked through.

**Nutrition:**

*Calorie: 400, Protein: 30g, Fat: 15g, Carb: 30g Calories: 250 Protein: 15g Carbs: 20g Fat: 12g*

# Zucchini Noodles & Turkey Bolognese

## Ingredients:

- 3 tbsps. olive oil
- 1 tbsps. minced garlic
- 2 tbsps. tomato paste
- 2 tsp sugar
- 3 medium zucchini
- 1/2 cup small diced onions
- 1-lb ground turkey
- 1 (28-oz.) can crushed tomatoes
- Parmesan cheese, for presenting

## Directions:

1. A big pan should have 2 tbsps of olive oil, garlic, and onions added to it. Cook for approximately 3 minutes at a middling temp.
2. After adding the ground turkey, raise the temp. to a medium level. You should include the crushed tomatoes, tomato paste, one teaspoon of salt, half a teaspoon of pepper, and two teaspoons of sugar once the turkey has been cooked.
3. Bring the temp. down to a low setting and continue cooking for approximately 10 minutes. A vegetable peeler or spiralizer can be used to chop the zucchini into noodles, which can then be used to make the zucchini noodles while the sauce is cooking.
4. Arrange the zucchini noodles on a plate, arrange the turkey bolognese on top of them, then sprinkle Parmesan cheese on top. Have a pleasant supper.

**Nutrition:**

*calories 270 protein 29 fat 13 carbs 11*

## Stuffed Portobello Mushrooms

### Ingredients

- 4 big Portobello mushrooms
- 1 cup quinoa
- ½ cup sundried tomatoes, chopped
- 1 cup mixed vegetables (e.g., spinach, bell peppers)
- ¼ cup olive oil
- Salt and pepperas required.

### Directions

1. Warm up the oven to 375 degF (190 degC). Clean mushrooms, removing stems.
2. put them on a baking sheet.
3. Cook quinoa as per to the package guidelines. In a pan, sauté vegetables and sundried tomatoes in olive oil.
4. Mix cooked quinoa with sautéed vegetables. Stuff each mushroom cap with the quinoa mixture.
5. Bake for 20-25 minutes until mushrooms are tender. Season with salt and pepper.

**Nutrition:**

Calorie: 350g Protein: 20g Fat: 10g Carb: 40g

# Chicken & Vegetable Stir-Fry

## Ingredients

- 300g fresh chicken breast, finely cut
- 2 cups mixed vegetables (bell peppers, broccoli, snap peas)
- ½ cup cashew nuts
- 2 tbsps soy sauce
- 1 tbsp olive oil
- 1 tsp ginger, minced
- 2 cloves garlic, curshed
- Salt and pepper as required.

## Directions

1. In a saucepan, bring the olive oil to a medium-high temp. Put chicken slices in the pan and heat them until they are browned and cooked through.
2. Move the chicken to one side of the pan and, if necessary, include additional oil to the pan. To create a fragrant aroma, sauté the ginger and garlic.
3. Include a variety of vegetables and stir-fry them until they are crunchy as well as tender.
4. Put the cashew nuts and soy sauce in the bowl. In order to mix all of the components, stir them together.
5. Salt and pepper should be added as required at this point.
6. Put the stir-fry on top of a bed of quinoa or brown rice that has been cooked

**Nutrition:**

Calorie: 420g Protein: 30g Fat: 15g Carb: 40g

# Baked Eggplant Parmesan

## Ingredients

- 1 small eggplant, cut into rounds
- ¼ cup marinara sauce
- ¼ cup shredded mozzarella cheese
- 1 tbsp grated Parmesan cheese
- ½ tbsp of olive oil
- A sprinkle of dried basil and oregano
- Salt and pepper as required.

## Directions

1. Warm up your oven to 375°F (190°C).
2. Brush the eggplant slices with olive oil and season with salt and pepper.
3. Put the eggplant slices on a baking pan and bake them for approximately 15 minutes, or until they reach the desired tenderness.
4. Take the eggplant out of the oven and place a dollop of marinara sauce, a sprinkle of mozzarella cheese, and a sprinkle of grated Parmesan cheese on top of each slice of eggplant.
5. Put the baking sheet back into the oven and continue baking for an extra 10 minutes, or until the cheese has melted and become bubbling around the edges.
6. With a side of mixed greens or a grain of your choice, serve the dish while it is still hot.

**Nutrition**

*calories 230, protein 10g, fat 14g, carbs 15g*

## CHICKEN AND VEGETABLE CASSEROLE

### INGREDIENTS

- 1 small chicken breast, diced
- 1 cup mixed vegetables (like broccoli, cauliflower, and carrots)
- 1/4 cup low-sodium chicken broth
- 1/2 tbsp olive oil
- 1/2 tbsp flour
- A sprinkle of dried thyme and rosemary
- Salt and pepper as required

### DIRECTIONS

1. Warm up your oven to 375 deg.F (190 deg.C).
2. Bring the olive oil to a simmer in a saucepan at a middling temp. Cook the chicken until it is no longer pink after adding the diced chicken.
3. Stir in the mixed vegetables, chicken broth, flour, dried thyme, dried rosemary, salt, and pepper. Transfer the mixture to an oven-safe casserole dish.
4. Cover the dish with aluminium foil and place it in the oven for approximately 20 minutes, or until the veggies are soft and the chicken is sufficiently cooked.
5. Present hot, as a complete meal.

### Nutrition

*calories 280, protein 30g, fat 12g, carbs 15g*

# Quinoa and Black Bean Tacos

## Ingredients

- ¼ cup cooked quinoa
- ¼ cup canned black beans, drained and washed.
- 2 small taco shells (corn or whole wheat)
- ¼ cup shredded lettuce
- ¼ cup diced tomatoes
- ¼ avocado, cut.
- Fresh cilantro leaves
- A squeeze of lime juice
- Salt and pepper as required.

## Directions

1. In a bowl, mix together the cooked quinoa and black beans. Season with salt and pepper.
2. Warm the taco shells in the oven or microwave.
3. Fill each taco shell with the quinoa and black bean mixture.
4. Top with shredded lettuce, diced tomatoes, cut avocado, and fresh cilantro leaves.
5. Drizzle with lime juice just before serving.
6. Present .hot, as a delicious and nutritious taco meal.

**Nutrition**

*calories 350, protein 10g, fat 15g, carbs 45g*

# Roasted Vegetable Pasta

## Ingredients

- ½ cup whole wheat pasta (or pasta of your choice)
- 1 cup mixed vegetables (like cherry tomatoes, zucchini, bell peppers)
- ½ tbsp of olive oil
- ½ tbsp balsamic vinegar
- A sprinkle of dried basil and oregano
- Salt and pepper as required
- 1 tbsp grated Parmesan cheese (optional)

## Directions

1. Warm up your oven to 400 deg.F (200 deg.C).
2. Toss the mixed vegetables in olive oil, balsamic vinegar, dried basil, dried oregano, salt, and pepper.
3. To roast the vegetables, spread them out in a single layer on a baking sheet and roast them for around 15 to 20 minutes, or until they are tender and have a mild caramelization.
4. While this is going on until the pasta is al dente, cook it per the directions on the package.
5. After draining the pasta, combine it with the veggies that have been roasted.
6. If preferred, sprinkle grated Parmesan cheese on top of the dish. Present hot, as a delightful pasta dish packed with roasted veggie goodness.

**Nutrition**

*calories 400, protein 12g, fat 15g, carbs 60*

# Teriyaki Chicken with Brown Rice

## Ingredients

- 1 small chicken breast, cut
- ¼ cup teriyaki sauce (store-bought or homemade)
- ½ cup cooked brown rice
- ¼ cup steamed broccoli florets
- ¼ cup sliced bell peppers
- ½ tbsp sesame seeds
- Salt and pepper as required.

## Directions

1. In a pan, cook the sliced chicken at a middling temp. until it's no longer pink and fully cooked.
2. After the chicken has been cooked, pour the teriyaki sauce over it and toss it all together until the chicken is all covered and the sauce is completely hot.
3. In a separate pot, cook the brown rice as per to the package instructions.
4. In a steamer or steamer basket, steam the broccoli florets and sliced bell peppers until they are tender-crisp.
5. present the teriyaki chicken over the cooked brown rice and garnish with steamed broccoli, bell peppers, and sesame seeds. Season with salt and pepper as desired.

**Nutrition**

*calories 400, protein 35g, fat 10g, carbs 45g*

# Hearty Vegetable Soup

## Ingredients

- 1 cup mixed vegetables (like carrots, celery, potatoes, peas)
- 1/4 onion, chopped
- 1/2 piece garlic, crushhed
- 1 cup vegetable broth
- 1/2 cup canned diced tomatoes (low-sodium)
- 1/2 tbsp olive oil
- A sprinkle of dried thyme and rosemary
- Salt and pepper as required.

## Direction

1. First, bring the olive oil to a simmer in a saucepan at a middling temp. Include the crushed garlic and chopped onion, and continue to sauté until the onion and garlic have become more tender.
2. Include the vegetables that have been combined together and continue to sauté for a couple of more minutes.
3. Pour the diced tomatoes from the can and the vegetable broth into the pot. Add some dried thyme and rosemary, along with some salt and pepper, as required.
4. After bringing the mixture to a boil, lower the temp. to a low setting and allow the soup to simmer for around 20 to 25 minutes, or until the vegetables are soft and the flavours have been thoroughly combined.
5. Present hot, as a comforting and nutritious soup.

**Nutrition**

*calories 180, protein 5g, fat 5g, carbs 30g*

# Snacks

## BAKED ZUCCHINI CHIPS

### INGREDIENTS

- 1 small zucchini, finely cut
- 1 tbsp olive oil
- 1/2 tbsp grated Parmesan cheese (optional, for added flavor)
- A pinch of garlic powder
- A pinch of salt and pepper

### DIRECTION

1. 1Line a baking sheet with parchment paper and warm up your oven to 375 deg.F (190 deg.C).
2. Put the zucchini slices that have been finely cut in a bowl and include olive oil, grated Parmesan cheese (if using), garlic powder, salt, and pepper. Toss the zucchini slices until they are uniformly covered with the mixture.
3. Organize the zucchini slices that have been seasoned in a single layer on the baking sheet that has been prepared.
4. Bake the zucchini chips for around 15 to 20 minutes, or until they have a golden undertone and a crisp texture.
5. Before you serve them, let them cool down a couple of degrees.
6. Present the baked zucchini chips as a nutritious and low-calorie alternative to regular potato chips.

**Nutrition**

*calories 150, protein 4g, fat 12g, carbs 10g*

## ROASTED CHICKPEAS

### INGREDIENTS

- 1 cup cooked chickpeas (canned or homemade, drained andwashed)
- ½ tbsp olive oil
- ½ tsp ground cumin
- ½ tsp smoked paprika
- ¼ tsp garlic powder
- ¼ tsp onion powder
- A pinch of cayenne pepper (optional, for a spicy kick)
- Salt and pepper as required.

### DIRECTION

1. Line a baking sheet with parchment paper and warm up your oven to 400 deg.F (200 deg.C).
2. Put the chickpeas that have been cooked in a bowl and thoroughly combine them with olive oil, ground cumin, smoked paprika, garlic powder, onion powder, cayenne pepper (if using), salt, and pepper. Toss the chickpeas until they are uniformly covered with the mixture.
3. Arrange the chickpeas that have been seasoned in a single layer on the baking sheet that has been prepared.
4. Roast the chickpeas in the oven for around 20 to 25 minutes, or until they have a golden and crispy texture.
5. Enjoy the roasted chickpeas as a crunchy and protein-packed snack or sprinkle them on top of salads for added texture and flavor.

**Nutrition**

*calories 200, protein 9g, fat 8g, carbs 25g*

# Mango Salsa with Tortilla Chips

## Ingredients:

- 1 ripe mango, diced
- 1/2 red bell pepper, diced
- 1/4 red onion, finely chopped
- 1 jalapeño pepper, seeded and crushed.
- Juice of 1 lime
- Handful of fresh cilantro, chopped
- Salt and pepper as required
- Tortilla chips for presenting

## Direction

1. In a bowl, include mango that has been diced, red bell pepper, red onion, jalapeño pepper, lime juice, and cilantro that has been cut.
2. Season with salt and pepper as required.
3. present with tortilla chips for dipping.
4. To alter the level of heat in the salsa, you can change the amount of jalapeño pepper by including more or less. For added flavor and texture, add diced avocado or pineapple.

**Nutrition:**

*Calories: 150 Protein: 3g Fat: 6g Carbs: 25g*

# Dark Chocolate and Almond Protein Bars

## Ingredients

- ½ cup almonds
- ¼ cup dark chocolate chips (preferably 70% cocoa or higher)
- ¼ cup almond butter
- ¼ cup protein powder (your choice of flavor)
- ¼ cup honey or maple syrup
- A pinch of salt

## Direction

1. In a food processor, blend the almonds, dark chocolate chips, almond butter, protein powder, honey (or maple syrup), and a pinch of salt until the mixture forms a sticky and crumbly texture.
2. Transfer the mixture to a square baking dish lined with parchment paper.
3. Press the mixture firmly into the dish to form a compact layer.
4. Refrigerate the dish for about 1-2 hours, or until the mixture is firm and easy to cut. Once set, cut the mixture into bars or squares.
5. Enjoy the dark chocolate and almond protein bars as a delicious and satisfying post-workout snack or an energy-boosting treat.

**Nutrition**

*calories 250, protein 10g, fat 15g, carbs 20g*

# Healthy Nut Butter Rice Cakes

## Ingredients

- 2 rice cakes (plain or lightly salted)
- 2 tbsps nut butter (such as almond, peanut, or cashew butter)
- ½ banana, finely cut
- ½ tbsp chia seeds
- A drizzle of honey (optional, for added sweetness)

## Direction

1. Spread one tbsp of nut butter on each rice cake.
2. Layer the finely cut banana on top of the nut butter.
3. Sprinkle chia seeds over the banana slices.
4. Optionally, drizzle a little honey over the rice cakes for added sweetness.
5. Enjoy the healthy nut butter rice cakes as a quick and satisfying snack for a boost of energy.

**Nutrition**

*calories 300, protein 7g, fat 15g, carbs 35g*

# Cucumber Rolls with Tuna Salad

## Ingredients:

- 1 cucumber
- 1 can tuna, drained
- 2 tbsps Greek yogurt or mayonnaise
- 1 tbsp Dijon mustard
- 1/4 cup diced celery
- 1/4 cup diced red onion
- Salt and pepper as required.

## Direction

1. Employing a vegetable peeler, cut the cucumber into several lengthy strips by slicing it very finely along its length.
2. In a bowl, mix tuna, Greek yogurt or mayonnaise, Dijon mustard, diced celery, and diced red onion.
3. Place a spoonful of tuna salad at one end of each cucumber strip.
4. Roll up the cucumber strip to form a tight roll. Secure with a toothpick if necessary.
5. Repeat with remaining cucumber strips and tuna salad.

**Nutrition:**

*Calories: 200 Protein: 20g Carbs: 10g Fat: 8g*

# Healthy Granola Bars

## Ingredients

- ½ cup rolled oats
- ¼ cup unsweetened shredded coconut
- ¼ cup chopped nuts (almonds, walnuts, or your favorite)
- ¼ cup dried fruit (raisins, cranberries, apricots, etc.)
- ¼ cup almond butter or peanut butter
- ¼ cup honey or maple syrup
- A pinch of salt

## Direction

1. In a mixing bowl, blend the rolled oats, shredded coconut, chopped nuts, and dried fruit.
2. In a small saucepan, gently warm the almond butter or peanut butter with honey (or maple syrup) and a pinch of salt until it's smooth and well combined.
3. Pour the almond butter mixture over the dry components and stir until everything is uniformly covered. In order to create a compact layer, push the mixture thoroughly into a baking dish that has been lined
4. Refrigerate the mixture for about 1-2 hours, or until it's set and firm. Once set, cut the mixture into bars or squares.
5. Present the healthy granola bars as an on-the-go snack or a quick energy boost during the day.

**Nutrition**

*calories 200, protein 5g, fat 10g, carbs 20g,*

# Smoked Salmon Cucumber Bites

## Ingredients

- 4 ounces smoked salmon
- 1 cucumber
- 4 tbsps cream cheese

## Direction

1. Peel the cucumber and slice it into rounds.
2. The second step is to spread a very fine layer of cream cheese on each cucumber circle.
3. Top with a small piece of smoked salmon.
4. Repeat for all cucumber rounds.

**Nutrition**

Calorie: 250 Protein: 20g Fat: 10g Carb: 20g

# Zucchini Fritters with Yogurt Sauce

### Ingredients:
- 2 medium zucchinis, grated
- 1/2 cup whole wheat flour or almond flour – 2 eggs
- 1/4 cup grated Parmesan cheese
- 2 cloves garlic, crushed.
- 1/4 tsp dried oregano
- Salt and pepper as required.
- Olive oil for frying
- 1/2 cup Greek yogurt
- 1 tbsp lemon juice
- Handful of fresh dill, chopped

### Direction
1. The zucchini should be grated and then placed in a clean kitchen towel. The excess moisture should be squeezed out.
2. The zucchini that has been grated, flour, eggs, Parmesan cheese, garlic, dried oregano, salt, and pepper should be mixed together in a big basin.
3. In a skillet, bring the olive oil to a temperature of medium. A spoonful of the zucchini mixture should be dropped into the skillet, and then the back of a spoon should be used to flatten it into fritters.
4. On all sides, heat for 3 to 4 minutes, or until the meat is golden brown and cooked through.
5. Meanwhile, mix Greek yogurt, lemon juice, and chopped dill in a small bowl to make the yogurt sauce. Present zucchini fritters hot with yogurt sauce on the side.

**Nutrition:**

*Calories: 250 Protein: 10g Fat: 12g Carbs: 20g Fiber: 4g*

# Banana-Oat Cookies

## Ingredients:
- 2 ripe bananas, mashed
- 1 cup rolled oats
- ¼ cup chopped nuts (e.g., almonds, walnuts)
- ¼ cup dried cranberries
- 1 tbsp honey
- ½ tsp vanilla extract
- ½ tsp ground cinnamon

## Direction
1. Warm up your oven to 350 deg.F (180 deg.C).
2. In a bowl, blend mashed bananas, rolled oats, chopped nuts, dried cranberries, honey, vanilla extract, and ground cinnamon.
3. Give everything a thorough mixing until it is completely combined.
4. Use the back of a spoon to softly flatten each biscuit.
5. Bake for 12-15 minutes until golden brown. Let the cookies cool before enjoying these guilt-free treats.

**Nutrition:**

*Calories: 120, Protein: 3g, Fat: 4g, Carbs: 20g*

# Baked Kale Chips

## Ingredients

- 1 cup kale leaves, torn into bite-sized pieces (stemstaken out)
- ½ tbsp olive oil
- ½ tbsp nutritional yeast (optional, for added flavor)
- A pinch of garlic powder
- A pinch of salt

## Direction

1. Line a baking sheet with parchment paper and warm up your oven to 300 deg.F (150 deg.C).
2. In a bowl, drizzle the torn kale leaves with olive oil and toss until the leaves are uniformly covered.
3. Sprinkle nutritional yeast (if using), garlic powder, and salt over the kale leaves and toss again.
4. Spread the kale leaves that have been seasoned out in a single layer on the baking sheet that has been prepared. Bake for about 10-15 minutes, or until the kale leaves are crispy but not burnt.
5. Allow them to cool mildly prior to presenting.
6. Present the baked kale chips as a guilt-free and nutrient-rich alternative to regular potato chips.

**Nutrition**

*calories 100, protein 4g, fat 7g, carbs 8g*

# Vanilla Protein Pancakes

## Ingredients:

- ½ cup oat flour
- 1 scoop vanilla protein powder
- ½ tsp baking powder
- ¼ tsp cinnamon
- ½ cup unsweetened almond milk
- 1 egg
- ½ tsp vanilla extract

**Nutrition**

Calories: 180, Protein: 15g Fat: 5g, Carbs: 20g,

## Directions

1. In a bowl, combine the oat flour, vanilla protein powder, baking powder, and cinnamon by whisking them together completely.
2. Put the egg, vanilla extract, and almond milk in a distinct basin and whisk them together.
3. After adding the wet components to the dry components, stir the mixture until it is completely incorporated.
4. Bring a skillet that does not stick to fire to a middling temp. Once the skillet is hot, pour a quarter cup of the pancake batter over it.
5. Cook the food until bubbles appear on the surface, then flip it over and continue cooking it until the second side is golden orange.
6. Proceed with the remaining batter. To accompany the vanilla protein pancakes, you can serve them with a drizzle of honey or fresh fruit.

# Dessert

## Homemade Trail Mix

### Ingredients

- 1/4 cup raw almonds
- 1/4 cup raw cashews
- 1/4 cup dried cranberries
- 1/4 cup pumpkin seeds
- 1/4 cup dark chocolate chips (preferably 70% cocoa or higher)
- A pinch of sea salt (optional, for added flavor)

### Direction

1. In a mixing bowl, blend the raw almonds, raw cashews, dried cranberries, pumpkin seeds, and dark chocolate chips.
2. Optionally, sprinkle a pinch of sea salt over the mixture for a sweet and salty flavor contrast.
3. Toss everything together until the ingredients are evenly distributed.
4. Store the homemade trail mix in an airtight container and enjoy it as a convenient and nutrient-packed snack on-the-go.

**Nutrition**

*calories 250, protein 6g, fat 18g, carbs 18g*

## Fresh Fruit Salad with Mint

### Ingredients

- ½ cup mixed fresh fruits (such as strawberries, blueberries, kiwi, mango, and grapes)
- ½ tbsp fresh lime or lemon juice
- ½ tbsp honey or maple syrup (optional, for added sweetness)
- Fresh mint leaves for garnish

### Direction

1. Wash, peel (if needed), and chop the fresh fruits into bite-sized pieces. In a bowl, toss the mixed fresh fruits with lime or lemon juice.
2. Optionally, drizzle honey (or maple syrup) over the fruit salad for added sweetness.
3. Garnish with fresh mint leaves just before serving.
4. Enjoy the refreshing and colorful fresh fruit salad as a light and nutritious dessert or snack.

**Nutrition**

*calories 100, protein 1g, fat 0g, carbs 25g*

## GREEK YOGURT WITH HONEY AND BERRIES

### INGREDIENTS

- 1 cup Greek yogurt (plain, unsweetened)
- ½ cup mixed berries (strawberries, blueberries, raspberries)
- ½ tbsp honey (optional, for added sweetness)
- A sprinkle of chopped nuts (like almonds or walnuts, optional)

### DIRECTION

1. In a bowl, scoop the Greek yogurt.
2. Top the yogurt with mixed berries and drizzle honey over the berries (if using).
3. Optionally, sprinkle some chopped nuts on top for added crunch and nutrition.
4. Enjoy the Greek yogurt with honey and berries as a refreshing and protein-rich breakfast or snack.

**Nutrition**

*calories 200, protein 12g, fat 8g, carbs 20g*

# Almond and Date Energy Bars

## Ingredients

- ½ cup almonds
- ½ cup dates, pitted
- ¼ cup unsweetened shredded coconut
- 1 tbsp almond butter
- A pinch of salt

## Direction

1. In a food processor, blend the almonds, dates that have been pitted, unsweetened shredded coconut, almond butter, and a pinch of salt. Blend the ingredients until the mixture reaches a consistency that is both sticky and crumbly.
2. Transfer the mixture to a square baking dish lined with parchment paper.
3. Press the mixture firmly into the dish to form a compact layer.
4. Refrigerate the dish for about 1-2 hours, or until the mixture is firm and easy to cut.
5. Once set, cut the mixture into bars or squares.
6. Enjoy the almond and date energy bars as a nutritious and energy-boosting snack throughout the day.

### Nutrition

*calories 200, protein 5g, fat 12g, carbs 20g*

# Cocoa Banana Bread

## Ingredients:

- 2 ripe bananas, mashed
- 1/4 cup coconut oil, melted
- 1/4 cup honey or maple syrup
- 2 eggs
- 1 tsp vanilla extract
- 1 3/4 cups whole wheat flour
- 1/4 cup unsweetened cocoa powder
- 1 tsp baking soda
- Pinch of salt Cooking

## Direction

1. Warm up the oven to 175 deg.C (350 deg.F). Prepare a loaf pan by greasing it with coconut oil or lining it with greaseproof paper.
2. Put the mashed bananas, the melted coconut oil, the honey or maple syrup, the eggs, and the vanilla essence into a big mixing bowl.
3. Meanwhile, in a distinct bowl, combine the cocoa powder, baking soda, salt, and whole wheat flour by whisking them together.
4. While mixing constantly, slowly include the dry components to the wet components until they are completely incorporated. After the loaf pan has been prepped, pour the batter into it and smooth up the top.
5. Bake the cake for 40 to 45 minutes, or until a toothpick inserted into the centre of the cake comes out clean.
6. After allowing the banana bread to cool for 10 minutes in the pan, move it to a wire rack to finish cooling entirely.

### Nutrition:

Calories: 180 Protein: 4g Fat: 7g Carbs: 28g

# Dark Chocolate Avocado Mousse

## Ingredients

- 2 ripe avocados
- ½ cup dark chocolate pieces (70% cocoa or higher)
- ¼ cup maple syrup
- 1 tsp vanilla extract
- A pinch of sea salt
- Fresh cherries, blueberries, and mint for garnish

## Directions

1. To begin, melt the dark chocolate by using either a microwave or a double boiler. Let it cool down a little bit.
2. Combine skinned avocados, melted chocolate, maple syrup, vanilla extract, and a pinch of sea salt in a blender.
3. Blend until smooth.
4. Spoon the mousse into individual serving bowls and in the fridge for almost 2 hours.
5. Garnish with fresh cherries, blueberries, and mint before serving.

**Nutrition**

*Calorie: 400 Protein: 20g Fat: 20g Carb: 40g*

## GREEK YOGURT POPSICLES WITH FRESH FRUIT

### INGREDIENTS

- 1 cup Greek yogurt (plain, unsweetened)
- 1/2 cup mixed fresh fruit (such as sliced strawberries, blueberries, and kiwi)
- 1 tbsp honey or maple syrup (optional, for added sweetness)

### DIRECTION

1. To begin, add the honey (or maple syrup) and Greek yoghurt in a bowl and stir until the two are thoroughly blended.
2. Layer the Greek yogurt mixture and the mixed fresh fruit in popsicle molds. Insert popsicle sticks into each mold.
3. Freeze the popsicles for almost 4 hours or until fully set.
4. Relish the Greek yogurt popsicles with fresh fruit as a refreshing and guilt-free dessert or a cool snack on a warm day.

**Nutrition**

*calories 150, protein 6g, fat 5g, carbs 20g*

## BAKED PEAR WITH WALNUTS & HONEY

### INGREDIENTS

- 4 ripe pears, divided and cored
- 1/2 cup walnuts, chopped
- 1/4 cup honey
- 1/2 cup ricotta cheese
- 1 tsp cinnamon

### DIRECTIONS

1. Warm up your oven to 375 deg.F (190 deg.C). Put pear halves, cut side up, on a baking sheet.
2. In a small bowl, mix chopped walnuts and cinnamon.
3. Sprinkle the walnut mixture over each pear half.
4. Drizzle honey over the pears in a uniform layer. Bake the pears for 25 minutes, or until they are soft and the walnuts have turned a golden colour.
5. Present each pear half with a dollop of ricotta cheese.

**Nutrition**

*Calorie: 320 Protein: 14g Fat: 14g Carb: 28g*

## APPLE CINNAMON BAKED OATMEAL CUPS

### INGREDIENTS

- 1 cup rolled oats
- 1 medium apple, grated or finely chopped
- ¼ cup chopped nuts (like walnuts or pecans)
- ½ tsp ground cinnamon
- 1 tbsp honey or maple syrup
- 1 cup milk (dairy or plant-based)
- 1 large egg
- ½ tsp vanilla extract
- A pinch of salt

### DIRECTION

1. Warm up your oven to 350 deg.F (175 deg.C) and line a muffin tin with paper liners.
2. In a mixing bowl, blend the rolled oats, grated or chopped apple, chopped nuts, ground cinnamon, and a pinch of salt.
3. Put the honey (or maple syrup), milk, egg, and vanilla extract in a distinct bowl and whisk all of the ingredients together.
4. Transfer the liquid mixture to the bowl containing the dry components, and whisk the mixture until it is thoroughly incorporated. In the muffin tray that has been prepared, distribute the ingredients in an even manner among the cups.
5. Bake for about 20-25 minutes, or until the oatmeal cups are set and lightly golden on top.
6. Allow them to cool slightly before removing from the muffin tin.
7. Enjoy the apple cinnamon baked oatmeal cups as a wholesome and portable breakfast or snack.

### Nutrition

*calories 200, protein 6g, fat 8g, carbs 25g*

# Peanut Butter & Jelly Protein Bars

## Ingredients

- 1 cup old-fashioned oats
- 1 cup protein powder (vanilla or peanut butter flavor)
- ½ cup natural peanut butter
- ¼ cup honey or maple syrup
- ¼ cup almond milk
- ½ cup strawberry jelly (no added sugar)

## Directions

1. In a bowl, blend oats and protein powder.
2. In a small saucepan, gently heat peanut butter, honey (or maple syrup), and almond milk until smooth.
3. Pour the peanut butter mixture over the oats and protein powder. Blend thoroughly . Press half of the mixture into a lined baking dish.
4. A layer of strawberry jelly should be poured on top of the cake. Crumble the rest of the oat mixture over the jelly, pressing gently.
5. Refrigerate for almost 2 hours before cutting into bars.

### Nutrition

calorie: 300 proteins: 20g fat: 10g carb: 40g

# Chocolate-Dipped Coconut Macaroons

## Ingredients

- 3 cups shredded coconut (unsweetened)
- 1 cup coconut flour
- 1 cup coconut oil (melted)
- ½ cup honey
- 1 tsp vanilla extract
- ½ tsp sea salt
- 200g dark chocolate (70% cocoa), chopped

### Nutrition

Calorie: 320 Protein: 14g Fat: 14g Carb: 28g

## Directions

1. Warm up your oven to 350 deg.F (175 deg.C) and line a baking sheet with parchment paper.
2. blend shredded coconut, coconut flour, melted coconut oil, honey, vanilla extract, and sea salt in a big bowl. After thoroughly combining, blend.
3. Scoop tbsp -sized portions and shape them into macaroons. Position them on the baking sheet that has been prepared.
4. Bake the edges for 15 minutes, or until they have a golden brown colour. Please allow them to completely cool off. The dark chocolate should be melted in a heatproof bowl over water that is simmering, or it can be melted in the microwave.
5. After each macaroon has cooled, you should dip the bottom of each macaroon into the melted chocolate and then set them back on the parchment paper. Sprinkle shredded coconut on top of each dipped macaroon.
6. Put in the fridge for 10 minutes or until the chocolate is set.

# Mango & Coconut Rice Pudding

## Ingredients

- 1 cup brown rice
- 2 cups coconut milk
- 1 ripe mango, diced
- ¼ cup shredded coconut
- 1 tbsp honey or maple syrup
- 1 tsp vanilla extract
- A pinch of salt

## Directions

1. Give the brown rice a thorough washing in a sink full of cold water.
2. Combine the rice, coconut milk, vanilla extract, and a pinch of salt in a saucepan. After bringing the mixture to a boil, decrease the temp. to a low setting, cover the pot, and let it simmer for 20 to 25 minutes, or until the rice is done.
3. Once the rice is cooked, stir in the honey or maple syrup. After removing it from the fire, cover it and let it sit for 5 minutes so that any liquid that may be left can be absorbed.
4. Mix the rice with a fork, fold the diced mango, and shred the coconut.
5. Present warm and enjoy the delightful flavors of Mango and Coconut Rice Pudding.

**Nutrition**

*Calorie: 320 Protein: 16g Fat: 16g Carb: 32g*

# CHAPTER 7
## FAQ Section for the GOLO Diet

This FAQ section is designed to address common questions and concerns that arise when following the GOLO diet. It aims to clarify aspects related to diet logistics, adaptations for special nutritional needs, and how to manage social situations while maintaining dietary guidelines. Here, we'll start by addressing three common queries.

**1. How do I start the GOLO diet if I have dietary restrictions such as gluten intolerance or lactose intolerance?**

Answer: Starting the GOLO diet with specific dietary restrictions involves careful planning to substitute certain foods while ensuring you receive all necessary nutrients. For gluten intolerance, replace wheat-based products with gluten-free grains like quinoa, rice, or gluten-free oats. For lactose intolerance, opt for lactose-free dairy or plant-based alternatives such as almond, soy, or oat milk. It's important to read labels carefully and consult a dietitian to ensure your diet remains balanced and aligned with the GOLO principles.

**2. How can I maintain my GOLO diet when eating out or attending social events?**

Answer: Maintaining the GOLO diet in social settings can be challenging but manageable with some planning. When eating out, look for menu items that are closest to the foods included in your diet plan, such as grilled meats, vegetables, and salads. Don't hesitate to ask for dishes to be prepared without added sugars or unhealthy fats. At social events, you can offer to bring a dish that fits your diet, ensuring you'll have something appropriate to eat. Communicating your dietary needs with hosts or restaurant staff can also help them provide options that meet your requirements.

**3. What should I do if I'm not seeing weight loss results with the GOLO diet?**

Answer: If you're not seeing the expected weight loss results, consider several factors before making adjustments.

First, ensure you're following the diet as recommended, including proper portion sizes and not skipping meals. The incorporation of consistent physical activity into your daily routine is also an essential component, which boosts metabolism and aids weight loss. If you're consistent with these practices but still not seeing results, consult with a healthcare provider or a dietitian. They can help assess your situation, suggest potential changes, or identify underlying issues that may be affecting your weight loss efforts.

## 4. Can the GOLO diet accommodate a vegetarian or vegan lifestyle?

Answer: Yes, the GOLO diet can be adapted for vegetarian or vegan lifestyles. The key is to substitute animal proteins with high-quality plant proteins such as lentils, chickpeas, tofu, and quinoa. These provide essential amino acids and other nutrients crucial for a balanced diet. Additionally, ensure you're getting enough iron, calcium, and vitamin B12, which are common nutrients of concern in vegetarian and vegan diets. Supplements might be necessary to meet these needs.

## 5. How does the GOLO diet address sugar cravings?

Answer: The GOLO diet helps manage sugar cravings by promoting a balanced intake of macronutrients, especially complex carbohydrates and proteins, which can stabilize blood sugar levels. Including healthy fats in your diet also helps enhance satiety, reducing the likelihood of cravings. Additionally, the GOLO diet encourages the consumption of whole fruits and some whole grains, which can satisfy a sweet tooth without spiking your blood sugar.

## 6. Is the GOLO diet suitable for people with type 2 diabetes?

Answer: The GOLO diet can be suitable for individuals with type 2 diabetes, but it should be followed under medical supervision. The diet's emphasis on balancing macronutrients and reducing intake of processed foods can help stabilize blood sugar levels. However, each person's dietary needs can vary based on their health status and medication regimen, so it's essential to consult with a healthcare professional before starting the diet to ensure it is appropriately tailored to your specific needs.

## 7. What are some tips for meal planning on the GOLO diet?

Answer: Effective meal planning on the GOLO diet involves preparing balanced meals that align with the diet's guidelines. Start by planning your meals around lean proteins, a variety of vegetables, and healthy fats. Batch cooking and prepping meals in advance can save time during the week. Additionally, having healthy snacks on hand, like nuts, seeds, and fresh fruit, can help you avoid unhealthy choices when you're hungry.

### 8. How can I track my progress on the GOLO diet?

Answer: Tracking progress on the GOLO diet involves more than just monitoring weight. It's also important to note changes in your energy levels, how your clothes fit, and any improvements in health markers like blood pressure and blood sugar levels. Keeping a food diary can help you stay committed and identify any areas where adjustments might be needed. For a more detailed analysis, consider using apps that track nutrition, activity, and overall health.

### 9. Can I follow the GOLO diet if I am pregnant or breastfeeding?

Answer: The GOLO diet can be adapted for pregnant or breastfeeding women, but it is essential to do so under the supervision of a healthcare professional. During these periods, nutritional needs increase, especially for nutrients like folic acid, iron, and calcium. It is important to ensure that the diet provides adequate caloric intake and is rich in vital nutrients to support both the mother and the child. Always consult with your doctor or a qualified dietitian before starting or modifying any dietary regimen during pregnancy or breastfeeding.

### 10. What are the main benefits of the GOLO diet besides weight loss?

Answer: Beyond weight loss, the GOLO diet aims to improve metabolism and stabilize blood insulin levels, which can lead to numerous health benefits. These include increased energy throughout the day, improvements in stress management and sleep, reduced risk of developing chronic diseases like type 2 diabetes, and improvements in cardiovascular health. Additionally, many followers of the diet report improvements in their skin and a reduction in inflammation due to the high quality and balance of nutrients promoted by the diet.

### 11. How can I manage feelings of hunger on the GOLO diet?

Answer: Feeling hungry can be a common challenge in the initial stages of any diet. The GOLO diet encourages eating balanced meals that include a good amount of protein, healthy fats, and complex carbohydrates to help maintain a feeling of fullness longer and stabilize blood sugar levels. It's also important to drink plenty of water, which can help reduce hunger. If feelings of hunger persist, it might be helpful to slightly increase your fiber intake through additional vegetables or incorporate healthy snacks like nuts or Greek yogurt, both of which are nutritious and filling.

## 12. Is the GOLO diet suitable for individuals with high cholesterol or heart conditions?

Answer: The GOLO diet can be suitable for individuals with high cholesterol or heart conditions as it focuses on balanced nutrition and encourages the intake of whole, unprocessed foods rich in fiber, lean proteins, and healthy fats. These dietary choices can help improve cholesterol levels and promote heart health. However, it's crucial to customize the diet to fit specific health needs and consult with a healthcare provider before starting the diet, especially if you have pre-existing health conditions or are on medication for heart issues.

## 13. Can the GOLO diet help with symptoms of hormonal imbalances, such as in PCOS or menopause?

Answer: Yes, the GOLO diet, which emphasizes balanced blood sugar levels through a healthy intake of macronutrients and micronutrients, can potentially help manage symptoms associated with hormonal imbalances like PCOS and menopause. The diet's focus on reducing processed foods and sugars and increasing nutrient-dense foods can improve insulin sensitivity, which is often a concern in PCOS, and help stabilize hormone levels affected by menopause. Nevertheless, individual results can vary, and it's advisable to work with a healthcare provider to tailor the diet to your specific hormonal health needs.

## 14. How long should I follow the GOLO diet to see significant results?

Answer: The time it takes to see significant results from the GOLO diet can vary depending on individual factors like diet adherence, starting weight, metabolism, and daily activity level. Generally, many people begin to see noticeable results within the first three to six weeks.

It's important to follow the diet consistently and incorporate regular physical activity to achieve the best results. Keeping a journal to track your progress, including dietary intake, exercise, and changes in weight and measurements, can also be helpful.

## 15. Are there any specific supplements recommended to complement the GOLO diet?

Answer: While the GOLO diet is designed to meet nutritional needs primarily through food, certain supplements may be recommended to support overall health, especially if specific nutrient deficiencies are known or suspected. Common supplements that might complement the GOLO diet include a high-quality multivitamin, omega-3 fatty acids, and possibly vitamin D if you have limited sun exposure or have been tested deficient. As always, consult with a healthcare professional before starting any new supplement regimen to ensure it's appropriate for your health conditions and diet.

**Inizio modulo**

# Conclusion

As we wrap up our look at the GOLO Diet Cookbook, it's evident that this journey can help us become healthier either you are just starting or a senior. The recipes provided are made to fit the GOLO Diet's rules, and eating nutritious foods can make a big difference in how we feel.

In this cookbook, we found quite a few yummy options for breakfast, lunch, and dinner. Each recipe is made with care to help us reach our health goals.  Whether it's a filling breakfast, a balanced dinner, or a tasty snack, these recipes are meant to support our efforts to manage our weight and feel better overall.

But the journey doesn't end here, it continues. As we bring these recipes into our daily lives, let's remember the importance of consistency. We can find what works best for us by experimenting with flavors and ingredients.  With dedication, we can tap into the power of the GOLO Diet to nourish our bodies and boost our energy. Let's embrace this journey and savor each step towards a healthier lifestyle.

# Recipe index

**Breakfast** .................................................................... 23
    Protein-Packed Omelette .............................................. 23
    Quinoa Breakfast Bowl ................................................ 23
    Banana Nut Overnight Oats ........................................... 24
    Veggie Breakfast Burrito ............................................... 25
    Overnight Oats with Berries .......................................... 25
    Egg and Veggie Scramble ............................................. 26
    Chia Pudding with Fruit ............................................... 27
    Avocado Toast on Whole Grain Bread ............................ 27
    Spinach and Feta Frittata ............................................. 28
    Healthy Banana Pancakes ............................................ 29
    Sweet Potato Hash ..................................................... 29
    Almond Milk and Oats Porridge .................................... 30

**Lunch** ........................................................................ 31
    Quinoa and Black Bean Stuffed Peppers ......................... 31
    Tuna Salad Stuffed Bell Peppers .................................... 31
    Black Bean and Corn Quesadillas .................................. 32
    Mushroom Barley Soup ............................................... 33
    Chicken and Avocado Wrap ......................................... 33
    Turkey Chili with Beans ............................................... 34
    Grilled Chicken Salad with Balsamic Vinaigrette ............... 35
    Veggie and Hummus Sandwich ..................................... 36
    Stuffed Bell Peppers ................................................... 37
    Spinach and Tomato Stuffed Chicken ............................. 37
    Sweet Potato and Black Bean Chili ................................ 38
    Veggie and Brown Rice Stir Fry ..................................... 39

**Dinner** ....................................................................... 40
    Grilled Beef Kebabs with Vegetables .............................. 40
    Cauliflower Fried Rice with Tofu .................................... 41
    Baked Lemon Herb Chicken with Quinoa ........................ 41
    Zucchini Noodles & Turkey Bolognese ........................... 42
    Stuffed Portobello Mushrooms ..................................... 43
    Chicken & Vegetable Stir-Fry ........................................ 44

Baked Eggplant Parmesan . . . . . . . . . . . . . . . . . . . . . . . . . . . . . . . . . . . . . . . . . . . . . . . . . . . . . . . . 44
Chicken and Vegetable Casserole . . . . . . . . . . . . . . . . . . . . . . . . . . . . . . . . . . . . . . . . . . . . . . .45
Quinoa and Black Bean Tacos . . . . . . . . . . . . . . . . . . . . . . . . . . . . . . . . . . . . . . . . . . . . . . . . .46
Roasted Vegetable Pasta . . . . . . . . . . . . . . . . . . . . . . . . . . . . . . . . . . . . . . . . . . . . . . . . . . . . .46
Teriyaki Chicken with Brown Rice . . . . . . . . . . . . . . . . . . . . . . . . . . . . . . . . . . . . . . . . . . . . .47
Hearty Vegetable Soup . . . . . . . . . . . . . . . . . . . . . . . . . . . . . . . . . . . . . . . . . . . . . . . . . . . . . .48

**Snacks** . . . . . . . . . . . . . . . . . . . . . . . . . . . . . . . . . . . . . . . . . . . . . . . . . . . . . . . . . . . . . . . . . . . . . .**49**
Baked Zucchini Chips . . . . . . . . . . . . . . . . . . . . . . . . . . . . . . . . . . . . . . . . . . . . . . . . . . . . . . . .49
Roasted Chickpeas . . . . . . . . . . . . . . . . . . . . . . . . . . . . . . . . . . . . . . . . . . . . . . . . . . . . . . . . . .50
Mango Salsa with Tortilla Chips . . . . . . . . . . . . . . . . . . . . . . . . . . . . . . . . . . . . . . . . . . . . . . 51
Dark Chocolate and Almond Protein Bars . . . . . . . . . . . . . . . . . . . . . . . . . . . . . . . . . . . . . 51
Healthy Nut Butter Rice Cakes . . . . . . . . . . . . . . . . . . . . . . . . . . . . . . . . . . . . . . . . . . . . . . .52
Cucumber Rolls with Tuna Salad . . . . . . . . . . . . . . . . . . . . . . . . . . . . . . . . . . . . . . . . . . . . .52
Healthy Granola Bars . . . . . . . . . . . . . . . . . . . . . . . . . . . . . . . . . . . . . . . . . . . . . . . . . . . . . . .53
Smoked Salmon Cucumber Bites . . . . . . . . . . . . . . . . . . . . . . . . . . . . . . . . . . . . . . . . . . . . .53
Zucchini Fritters with Yogurt Sauce . . . . . . . . . . . . . . . . . . . . . . . . . . . . . . . . . . . . . . . . . . .54
Banana-Oat Cookies . . . . . . . . . . . . . . . . . . . . . . . . . . . . . . . . . . . . . . . . . . . . . . . . . . . . . . . .55
Baked Kale Chips . . . . . . . . . . . . . . . . . . . . . . . . . . . . . . . . . . . . . . . . . . . . . . . . . . . . . . . . . . .56
Vanilla Protein Pancakes . . . . . . . . . . . . . . . . . . . . . . . . . . . . . . . . . . . . . . . . . . . . . . . . . . . .56

**Dessert** . . . . . . . . . . . . . . . . . . . . . . . . . . . . . . . . . . . . . . . . . . . . . . . . . . . . . . . . . . . . . . . . . . . . . . .**57**
Homemade Trail Mix . . . . . . . . . . . . . . . . . . . . . . . . . . . . . . . . . . . . . . . . . . . . . . . . . . . . . . . .57
Fresh Fruit Salad with Mint . . . . . . . . . . . . . . . . . . . . . . . . . . . . . . . . . . . . . . . . . . . . . . . . . .57
Greek Yogurt with Honey and Berries . . . . . . . . . . . . . . . . . . . . . . . . . . . . . . . . . . . . . . . . .58
Almond and Date Energy Bars . . . . . . . . . . . . . . . . . . . . . . . . . . . . . . . . . . . . . . . . . . . . . . .59
Cocoa Banana Bread . . . . . . . . . . . . . . . . . . . . . . . . . . . . . . . . . . . . . . . . . . . . . . . . . . . . . . .59
Dark Chocolate Avocado Mousse . . . . . . . . . . . . . . . . . . . . . . . . . . . . . . . . . . . . . . . . . . . .60
Greek Yogurt Popsicles with Fresh Fruit . . . . . . . . . . . . . . . . . . . . . . . . . . . . . . . . . . . . . . . 61
Baked Pear with Walnuts & Honey . . . . . . . . . . . . . . . . . . . . . . . . . . . . . . . . . . . . . . . . . . . 61
Apple Cinnamon Baked Oatmeal Cups . . . . . . . . . . . . . . . . . . . . . . . . . . . . . . . . . . . . . . .62
Peanut Butter & Jelly Protein Bars . . . . . . . . . . . . . . . . . . . . . . . . . . . . . . . . . . . . . . . . . . .63
Chocolate-Dipped Coconut Macaroons . . . . . . . . . . . . . . . . . . . . . . . . . . . . . . . . . . . . . . .63
Mango & Coconut Rice Pudding . . . . . . . . . . . . . . . . . . . . . . . . . . . . . . . . . . . . . . . . . . . . .64

# 60-DAY MEAL PLAN

Embarking on a journey toward better health and weight management with the GOLO diet requires a well-structured meal plan that not only focuses on weight loss but also enhances metabolic health and overall well-being. The 60-Day Meal Plan for the GOLO diet has been meticulously designed to integrate seamlessly into daily life, ensuring it is not only effective but also sustainable and enjoyable.

The essence of the GOLO diet revolves around balancing hormone levels, specifically insulin, to optimize metabolic health, which in turn aids in reducing body fat and increasing energy levels. This approach addresses the root causes of weight gain and metabolic distress, rather than just the symptoms. By focusing on nutrient-dense, whole foods that stabilize blood sugar levels and reduce inflammation, the diet aims to repair metabolic dysfunction.

The 60-day meal plan is crafted to introduce variety and balance, ensuring that meals are not repetitive and provide all essential nutrients needed for a healthy body. Each day is structured with three main meals—breakfast, lunch, and dinner—complemented by nutritious snacks to keep energy levels stable throughout the day. This rhythmic eating pattern helps to sustain satiety and prevent blood sugar spikes and dips, which are often responsible for cravings and overeating.

Breakfast options are designed to kickstart the metabolism with a mix of high-quality proteins, healthy fats, and carbohydrates. These meals are substantial enough to fuel morning activities but balanced to ensure they don't contribute to mid-morning slumps. Lunches are crafted to provide a midday boost with lean proteins and plenty of fresh vegetables, maintaining energy levels and focus into the afternoon. Dinners are centered around wholesome ingredients that support nighttime metabolism and promote good sleep, crucial for overall health and weight loss.

Moreover, the plan is flexible and considers different dietary needs and preferences. It includes options for vegetarians, those with specific dietary restrictions such as gluten or lactose intolerance, and adapts to different life stages and activity levels. This flexibility ensures that the meal plan can fit into any lifestyle, making it easier to adopt and stick to long term.

With this comprehensive and carefully structured meal plan, the GOLO diet not only encourages healthy weight loss but also promotes a lifestyle change towards eating whole, unprocessed foods. This shift not only supports metabolic health and energy levels but also enhances overall life quality, proving that a well-thought-out diet plan can indeed be a cornerstone of lifelong health and vitality.

# Weak 1

| Day | Breakfast | Dinner | Lunch | A.m/P.m Snack |
|---|---|---|---|---|
| Monday | High protein breakfast | Seafood with a side of vegetables (e.g., baked salmon with roasted Brussels sprouts) | Lean protein salad (e.g., grilled chicken salad with mixed greens and vinaigrette) | Greek yogurt with berries |
| Tuesday | Smoothie with protein powder, mixed berries, and spinach | Soup and sandwich (e.g., tomato basil soup with a turkey breast sandwich on whole grain bread) | Vegetarian dish (e.g., chickpea and vegetable curry) | A handful of nuts |
| Wednesday | Oatmeal with sliced almonds and apple chunks | Quinoa and roasted vegetable bowl with a lemon-tahini dressing | Lean meat (e.g., grilled lean steak with a side of sweet potato and green beans) | Carrot sticks with hummus |
| Thursday | Greek yogurt with granola and honey | Chicken Caesar salad | Fish tacos with cabbage slaw | An orange or any whole fruit |
| Friday | Protein pancakes with fresh berries | Beef and vegetable stir-fry | Pasta with a light tomato sauce and a side salad | Cottage cheese with pineapple |
| Saturday | Avocado toast with poached eggs | Tuna salad stuffed in whole wheat pita | Pork chops with apple sauce and steamed broccoli | Sliced cucumber with a sprinkle of chili and lime |
| Sunday | Breakfast burrito (eggs, low-fat cheese, peppers, onions, and salsa) | Lentil soup with a side of whole-grain bread | Roast chicken with quinoa and mixed vegetables | Mixed berries with a dollop of whipped cream |

# Weak 2

| Day | Breakfast | Dinner | Lunch | A.m/P.m Snack |
|---|---|---|---|---|
| Monday | French toast with whole grain bread and a side of mixed berries | Spinach and feta stuffed chicken breast with a side of couscous | Shrimp stir-fry with a variety of colorful bell peppers and brown rice | Apple slices with almond butter |
| Tuesday | Chia seed pudding topped with kiwi and coconut flakes | Turkey meatballs with spaghetti squash and marinara sauce | Grilled lamb chops with mint yogurt sauce and steamed asparagus | A small bowl of mixed nuts |
| Wednesday | Cottage cheese with pineapple and a sprinkle of cinnamon | Roast beef wrap with arugula, sun-dried tomatoes, and horseradish sauce | Baked cod with a lemon herb crust, served with quinoa salad | Greek yogurt topped with honey and walnuts |
| Thursday | Smoothie bowl with spinach, banana, protein powder, and a tbsp of flaxseeds | Quiche with a potato crust filled with broccoli and sharp cheddar | Pork tenderloin medallions with apple sauce and roasted sweet potatoes | Raw carrots and cucumber with hummus |
| Friday | Omelette with goat cheese, tomatoes, and fresh basil | Lentil soup with a side of whole grain garlic bread | Grilled tuna steak with a side of Mediterranean chickpea salad | Fresh figs with ricotta cheese |
| Saturday | Buckwheat pancakes topped with fresh strawberries and a drizzle of maple syrup | Chicken Caesar wrap using a whole grain tortilla | Vegetarian chili served with a side of cornbread | An orange and a handful of almonds |
| Sunday | Berry parfait with layers of granola, vanilla yogurt, and mixed berries | Grilled vegetable and hummus flatbread | Roast duck with cherry sauce and a side of braised red cabbage | Dark chocolate square and a pear |

# Weak 3

| Day | Breakfast | Dinner | Lunch | A.m/P.m Snack |
|---|---|---|---|---|
| **Monday** | Scrambled eggs with smoked salmon and chives | Quinoa and black bean salad with avocado, tomato, and lime dressing | Chicken tikka masala with cauliflower rice | Cottage cheese with sliced peaches |
| **Tuesday** | Overnight oats with banana slices and peanut butter | Beef and vegetable stir-fry with tamari sauce and sesame seeds | Grilled branzino with steamed green beans and almonds | A bowl of blueberries |
| **Wednesday** | Yogurt with granola and a drizzle of agave nectar | Spicy lentil soup with a side of whole-grain bread | Baked trout with herb butter and a quinoa and parsley salad | Sliced pear with a handful of walnuts |
| **Thursday** | Yogurt with granola and a drizzle of agave nectar | Spicy lentil soup with a side of whole-grain bread | Baked trout with herb butter and a quinoa and parsley salad | Sliced pear with a handful of walnuts |
| **Friday** | French toast with whole grain bread and a side of honey-roasted figs | Sliced turkey and avocado salad with a mustard vinaigrette | Vegetable lasagna with layers of eggplant, zucchini, and ricotta | Greek yogurt with a sprinkle of chia seeds |
| **Saturday** | Protein pancakes with a topping of almond butter and sliced bananas | Grilled shrimp Caesar salad with homemade whole grain croutons | Beef stroganoff served with spiralized zucchini noodles | An apple with a slice of cheddar cheese |
| **Sunday** | Baked avocado egg boats with crumbled feta and diced tomatoes | Roasted beet and goat cheese arugula salad | Lemon and herb roasted chicken with a side of mashed sweet potatoes | Homemade trail mix with almonds, dried cranberries, and pumpkin seeds |

# Weak 4

| Day | Breakfast | Dinner | Lunch | A.m/P.m Snack |
|---|---|---|---|---|
| Monday | Spinach and feta omelette with whole grain toast | Chicken and avocado wrap with whole wheat tortilla and light mayo | Seared salmon with a dill yogurt sauce and a side of roasted asparagus | Mixed nuts and dried fruits |
| Tuesday | Steel-cut oats with sliced strawberries and a dash of cinnamon | Grilled halloumi cheese salad with tomatoes, cucumbers, and olives | Moroccan lamb tagine with apricots and served with couscous | Celery sticks with almond butter |
| Wednesday | Mango and coconut milk smoothie | Turkey chili with a variety of beans and topped with low-fat sour cream | Grilled tilapia with a tropical salsa of pineapple and mango, served with wild rice | Greek yogurt with a drizzle of honey and a sprinkle of granola |
| Thursday | Poached eggs on a bed of sautéed greens with garlic | Beef pho with a rich bone broth, finely cut beef, and noodles | Chicken parmigiana with a side of spaghetti squash | A banana with a handful of sunflower seeds |
| Friday | Blueberry pancakes made with almond flour and topped with fresh blueberries | Asian sesame chicken salad with mandarin oranges, almonds, and sesame dressing | Pork chops with apple compote and steamed green peas | Carrot and cucumber slices with tzatziki dip |
| Saturday | Avocado and salmon on rye bread with a sprinkle of capers and red onion | Roasted vegetable and quinoa bowl with a lemon tahini dressing | Beef and broccoli stir-fry with garlic and soy sauce, served with brown rice | Cottage cheese with sliced kiwi |
| Sunday | Smoothie bowl with bananas, blueberries, spinach, and a spoonful of peanut butter | Mediterranean chickpea salad with olive oil and lemon dressing | Baked chicken thighs with Mediterranean herbs and a side of roasted Mediterranean vegetables | An orange and a few dark chocolate squares |

GOLO DIET COOKBOO

# Weak 5

| Day | Breakfast | Dinner | Lunch | A.m/P.m Snack |
|---|---|---|---|---|
| **Monday** | Greek yogurt with sliced almonds and fresh raspberries | Spicy black bean taco salad with grilled corn, avocado, and salsa | Roasted duck breast with a balsamic cherry reduction and wild rice pilaf | A pear and a small handful of walnuts |
| **Tuesday** | Scrambled tofu with spinach, mushrooms, and tomatoes | Grilled vegetable panini with pesto on whole grain bread | Herb-crusted cod with steamed broccoli and a lemon butter sauce | Hummus with sliced bell peppers and cucumber |
| **Wednesday** | Smoothie with banana, spinach, protein powder, and a spoonful of flaxseeds | Chicken Caesar salad with homemade whole grain croutons and light Caesar dressing | Vegetarian lasagna made with layers of zucchini, eggplant, and low-fat ricotta | An apple with a small piece of sharp cheddar cheese |
| **Thursday** | Overnight oats with coconut milk, chia seeds, and fresh mango | Roast beef and arugula sandwich with horseradish sauce on rye bread | Grilled shrimp over a bed of mixed greens with a vinaigrette dressing | A small bowl of mixed berries |
| **Friday** | Whole grain waffles with a light drizzle of maple syrup and sliced strawberries | Quinoa and roasted sweet potato salad with dried cranberries and a citrus dressing | Pan-seared salmon with a cucumber dill salad and quinoa | Greek yogurt with a sprinkle of cinnamon and a tsp of honey |
| **Saturday** | Avocado and egg toast on whole grain bread | Spicy lentil and kale soup | Chicken stir-fry with a variety of vegetables and a soy-ginger sauce, served with brown rice | Cottage cheese with sliced peaches |
| **Sunday** | Berry parfait with layers of granola, plain yogurt, and mixed fresh berries | Mediterranean chickpea wrap with lettuce, tomato, and tzatziki sauce | Beef stew with root vegetables and a side of whole grain bread | A handful of almonds and a few dried apricots |

GOLO DIET COOKBOO

# Weak 6

| Day | Breakfast | Dinner | Lunch | A.m/P.m Snack |
|---|---|---|---|---|
| Monday | Banana pancakes made with almond flour and topped with a dollop of Greek yogurt | Grilled chicken and avocado salad with mixed greens and a balsamic glaze | Thai green curry with tofu and a variety of vegetables served over jasmine rice | A handful of pistachios |
| Tuesday | Smoothie bowl with açai, banana, and a mix of tropical fruits topped with coconut flakes | Bulgur wheat tabbouleh with chopped parsley, tomatoes, and cucumber | Grilled trout with lemon and herbs, served with a side of sautéed spinach | Carrot sticks with a tahini dip |
| Wednesday | Oatmeal cooked with apple slices and cinnamon, topped with a sprinkle of nutmeg | Turkey and spinach wrap with cranberry sauce and whole grain tortilla | Lamb kebabs with bell peppers and onions, served with a side of Greek salad | A small bowl of cottage cheese with sliced grapes |
| Thursday | Eggs Benedict with smoked salmon on whole grain English muffins | Chickpea and roasted beet salad with goat cheese and walnuts | Beef bourguignon served over whole grain pasta | An orange and a few dark chocolate squares |
| Friday | Chia seed pudding flavored with vanilla and topped with fresh mango slices | Baked falafel with a side of hummus and pita bread | Roasted chicken breast with garlic and rosemary, served with a quinoa and arugula salad | Sliced kiwi and strawberries |
| Saturday | French omelette with mushrooms, tomatoes, and onions | Lentil soup with a drizzle of olive oil and a slice of rustic bread | Grilled pork tenderloin with a plum sauce, served with roasted brussels sprouts | Greek yogurt with a spoonful of almond butter |
| Sunday | Protein smoothie with spinach, blueberries, and a scoop of protein powder | Quinoa stuffed bell peppers with a mix of vegetables and spices | Duck confit with a side of mashed sweet potatoes and steamed green beans | A handful of mixed nuts |

# Weak 7

| Day | Breakfast | Dinner | Lunch | A.m/P.m Snack |
|---|---|---|---|---|
| Monday | Greek yogurt with sliced bananas and a drizzle of honey | Soba noodle salad with edamame, shredded carrots, and a sesame ginger dressing | Roasted turkey breast with cranberry sauce and a side of roasted butternut squash | A small bowl of mixed berries |
| Tuesday | Cottage cheese with sliced peaches and a sprinkle of flax seeds | Spiced chickpea stew with spinach and tomatoes served with a side of whole-wheat pita | Baked sea bass with a Mediterranean salsa of olives, capers, and tomatoes, served with wild rice | Celery sticks with almond butter |
| Wednesday | Smoothie with mixed greens, pineapple, and coconut water | Roast beef sandwich with horseradish mayo on whole grain bread | Stir-fried tofu with broccoli, bell peppers, and a soy sauce glaze, served over brown rice | A handful of raw almonds |
| Thursday | Scrambled eggs with diced bell peppers and onions, served on whole-grain toast | Quinoa salad with diced cucumber, cherry tomatoes, feta cheese, and a lemon olive oil dressing | Grilled lamb chops with mint pesto, served with a side of steamed green beans | Greek yogurt with a sprinkle of cinnamon |
| Friday | Muesli with skim milk, topped with fresh blueberries | Turkey and avocado wrap with a light ranch dressing | Pan-seared duck breast with a balsamic fig reduction, served with a side of mashed cauliflower | Sliced apple with a peanut butter dip |
| Saturday | Oatmeal cooked with almond milk, topped with sliced strawberries and a dash of vanilla extract | Balsamic glazed chicken breast with a spinach and walnut salad | Grilled shrimp over a salad of arugula, avocado, and grapefruit with a citrus vinaigrette | A small bowl of cottage cheese with pineapple chunks |
| Sunday | Poached eggs over a bed of sautéed kale and whole grain toast | Lentil and vegetable soup with a side of spelt bread | Beef stroganoff made with Greek yogurt instead of sour cream, served over whole grain egg noodles | A banana and a handful of walnuts |

# Weak 8

| Day | Breakfast | Dinner | Lunch | A.m/P.m Snack |
|---|---|---|---|---|
| **Monday** | Baked avocado eggs, topped with crumbled bacon and chives | Baked avocado eggs, topped with crumbled bacon and chives | Grilled salmon with a dill and lemon yogurt sauce, served with roasted parsnips | A handful of dried figs and almonds |
| **Tuesday** | Coconut yogurt with granola and a drizzle of agave syrup | Grilled chicken gyro with tzatziki sauce, wrapped in a whole wheat pita | Vegetable stir-fry with tofu, bok choy, and a spicy hoisin sauce, served over jasmine rice | Carrot and celery sticks with a blue cheese dip |
| **Wednesday** | Protein smoothie with kale, banana, almond milk, and a tbsp of peanut butter | Spicy black bean and corn burritos with salsa verde | Roast chicken with garlic and herbs, served with a quinoa and cranberry salad | Greek yogurt with sliced kiwi |
| **Thursday** | Steel-cut oats with fresh apple slices, cinnamon, and a touch of honey | Turkey meatloaf with a side of mashed sweet potatoes and steamed green beans | Baked haddock with a herb crust, served with a side of steamed asparagus and baby carrots | A pear and a small chunk of gorgonzola cheese |
| **Friday** | Scrambled eggs with smoked salmon, capers, and red onions | Lentil salad with roasted beets, goat cheese, and arugula, dressed with balsamic vinaigrette | Pork tenderloin in a mustard sauce, served with braised red cabbage | A small bowl of mixed berries with a dollop of whipped cream |
| **Saturday** | A small bowl of mixed berries with a dollop of whipped cream | Lentil salad with roasted beets, goat cheese, and arugula, dressed with balsamic vinaigrette | Pork tenderloin in a mustard sauce, served with braised red cabbage | A small bowl of mixed berries with a dollop of whipped cream |
| **Sunday** | French toast made with whole grain bread, topped with fresh berries and a light dusting of powdered sugar | Grilled vegetable and hummus wrap in a spinach tortilla | Beef chili with kidney beans, topped with a sprinkle of cheddar cheese and a dollop of sour cream | Sliced cucumbers and cherry tomatoes with a ranch dip |

# Weak 9

| Day | Breakfast | Dinner | Lunch | A.m/P.m Snack |
|---|---|---|---|---|
| **Monday** | Chia pudding made with almond milk and topped with sliced bananas and cocoa nibs | Chicken Caesar salad with romaine lettuce, parmesan shavings, and whole grain croutons | Seafood paella with shrimp, mussels, and saffron rice | A small bowl of cottage cheese with pineapple chunks |
| **Tuesday** | Smoothie with blueberries, spinach, Greek yogurt, and a tsp of flaxseed oil. | Roasted turkey breast with cranberry sauce and a side of sweet potato mash. | Grilled swordfish with a mango salsa, served with a side of cilantro lime rice. | A small bowl of air-popped popcorn sprinkled with nutritional yeast. |
| **Wednesday** | Whole grain waffles with almond butter and sliced bananas. | Spinach and feta stuffed portobello mushrooms with a side of couscous salad. | Lamb stew with root vegetables and a side of whole grain bread. | Sliced apples with a homemade cinnamon nutmeg dip. |
| **Thursday** | Cottage cheese with sliced peaches and a drizzle of honey. | Grilled shrimp salad with mixed greens, avocado, and a vinaigrette dressing | Beef bourguignon served over mashed cauliflower. | A handful of raw carrots and bell pepper strips with hummus. |
| **Friday** | Eggs Benedict with whole grain English muffins and smoked salmon. | Quinoa and black bean burger with a side of baked sweet potato fries. | Chicken curry with mixed vegetables served over basmati rice. | Greek yogurt topped with a spoonful of raspberry preserves and crushed pistachios. |

Printed in Great Britain
by Amazon